D1007819

"The noble chile—and its equally noble growers—illustrates the key principle we need for a world stressed by an ever-more-fickle climate: *resilience*. This book will make you understand the situation far better than most dry tomes on the subject."

—BILL MCKIBBEN, author of *Eaarth*, founder of 350.org

"This book will fascinate not only chile aficionados, but also those students of biodiversity who are alarmed at the disastrous effect that climate change is wreaking on our food crops in general. With this book in hand, I happily climbed aboard the authors' Spice Ship to embark on their personal odyssey, and saw up close the devastating effects of climate change on the environment, farmers, and their crops whose very existence is at stake."

—DIANA KENNEDY, author of *The Essential Cuisines of Mexico* and *The Art of Mexican Cooking*

"A treasure trove of chile lore and a wake-up call to everyone who cares about real food, *Chasing Chiles* will amuse and alarm you. These three gastronauts carry a wealth of culinary and botanical knowledge, and their journeys in their Spice Ship uncover an incredibly diverse world of chiles that is changing with breathtaking speed. Stop worrying about the impact of climate change on future harvests; cross your fingers for this year's instead."

—ROWAN JACOBSON, author of *American Terroir* and *Fruitless Fall*

"*Chasing Chiles* is truly one of the most inspiring and unique treatments of climate change in current literature. . . . And the proposed solution to this complex problem is both plain and prudent: 'Eat and farm as if the earth matters, as we should have been doing all along.'"

—FREDERICK KIRSCHENMANN, Distinguished Fellow, Leopold Center for Sustainable Agriculture, and president of Stone Barns Center for Food and Agriculture

"This book is an agri-culinary-eco-botanical odyssey that brings some of the most important issues about food, eating, and the impact of climate change to the fore in a way that is both engaging and compelling. A truly pleasurable read for anyone who appreciates authentic flavors and the pleasures of the table—and, of course, the wisdom of our farmers."

—TRACEY RYDER, CEO, Edible Communities

"How can our hemisphere's "spice of life" be ignored after reading *Chasing Chiles*? I mean, what will there be to live for?"

—WES JACKSON, president, The Land Institute

"An instant classic of chile pepper lore, *Chasing Chiles* is the best social history of chiles since Amal Naj's *Peppers* from 1992. In fact, I think it's better—because it's not just journalism; it has fascinating science and entertaining humor as well. Highly recommended!"

—DAVE DEWITT, "The Pope of Peppers" and coauthor of *The Complete Chile Pepper Book*

"*Chasing Chiles* is nothing short of a brilliant ethno-bio-culinary convergence. It accomplishes what so very few books do—marrying place to flavor and science—and the result is a visceral understanding of the profound impact climate change has on the global community and the foods that we always seem to take for granted. Kurt Friese, Kraig Kraft, and Gary Nabhan have produced a must-read classic for all time."

—ELISSA ALTMAN, author of *Poor Man's Feast*

# Chasing Chiles

# Chasing Chiles

## HOT SPOTS ALONG THE PEPPER TRAIL

## Kurt Michael Friese, Kraig Kraft, and Gary Paul Nabhan

CHELSEA GREEN PUBLISHING

WHITE RIVER JUNCTION, VERMONT

Project Manager: Patricia Stone
Editorial Contact: Makenna Goodman
Developmental Editor: Benjamin Watson
Copy Editor: Laura Jorstad
Proofreader: Nancy Ringer
Indexer: Lee Lawton
Designer: Peter Holm, Sterling Hill Productions
Photographs by the authors, as credited
Chile pepper illustration by Jean Andrews, from *The Pepper Trail*, published by the University of North Texas
    Press. We gratefully acknowledge the artistry of the late Dr. Jean Andrews for the title page and chapter art;
    she was one of the most passionate chile pepper scholars who ever lived.

Printed in the United States of America
First printing February, 2011
10 9 8 7 6 5 4 3      18 19 20 21

**Library of Congress Cataloging-in-Publication Data**
Friese, Kurt Michael.
Chasing chiles : hot spots along the pepper trail / Kurt Michael
Friese, Kraig Kraft, and Gary Paul Nabhan.
    p. cm.
Includes index.
ISBN 978-1-60358-250-6
1. Hot peppers. 2. Hot peppers--Climatic factors. 3. Endangered
plants--United States. 4. Endangered plants--Mexico. I. Kraft, Kraig.
II. Nabhan, Gary Paul. III. Title.
SB307.P4F75 2011
641.3'384--dc22

                                    2010049066

Chelsea Green Publishing
85 North Main Street, Suite 120
White River Junction, VT 05001
(802) 295-6300

www.chelseagreen.com

To our wives, Kim McWane Friese,
Heather Zornetzer, and Laurie Smith Monti

# CONTENTS

# ACKNOWLEDGMENTS

FIRST AND FOREMOST, we are grateful to our wives, Kim McWane Friese, Laurie Smith Monti, and Heather Zornetzer, for their companionship, encouragement, and patience while we were on phases of this spice odyssey. We are also indebted to our good friend and editor Ben Watson for constant insights and support. Margo Baldwin, Joni Praded, and others at Chelsea Green have been more than business partners as well; they have been allies for the same causes. Regina Fitzsimmons and Deja Walker, both of them interns with the Renewing America's Food Traditions alliance, have been part of our field team, as has Pat Friese, lexicographer and food historian. We have benefited from the work of many farmers, gardeners, chefs, food historians, and scientists along the way. Elders in the world of chiles—from the late Jean Andrews and late Charles Heiser, both of whom departed during the course of this project, to Dave DeWitt, Hardy Eshbaugh, Diana Kennedy, Paul Bosland, Clifford Wright, and Nancy and Jeff Gerlach—have offered us much inspiration over the years. Younger chile researchers, from Kimberlee Chambers, Susan Wesland, Jorge Carlos Berny Mier y Teran, Josh Tewksbury, Isaura Andaluz, and Charles Martin to Eric Votava and John Tuxill, have also been generous in sharing their knowledge with us.

We are also indebted to many others, listed here chapters by chapter:

*Sonora and Arizona:* Jesús and Casimiro Sanchez, Maria del Carmen Sanchez, Chata Gallego, Jeanie Neubauer, Alberto Búrquez, Angela Martinez, Anabela Carlón Flores, Angel Cota, Sergio Araújo, Oscar González, Chano, Fernando Niño Estudillo, Hugo Sesta, Kimberlee Chambers, Luis Córdoba, and Manuel López.

*Florida:* Bill and Bryanne Hamilton, Jean Dowdy and Pat Hamilton, Johnny Barnes, Richard "Cheech" Villadoniga, David Nolan, Mark

Barnes, Marcia and Steve McQuaig, Randy Haire, chef David Bearl and Eddie Lambert, Scott Carlson, and Mike Martin.

*Yucatán:* Nancy and Jeff Gerlach, John and Christine Piet, Jorge Carlos Berny Mier y Teran, Eugene Anderson, John Tuxill, and the many Mayan farmers we met in their fields and gardens.

*Louisiana:* Poppy Tooker, Harold Osborn, Shane K. Bernard, Mike Sarabian, Paul McIlhenny, Donald Link, Stephen Stryjewski, Leah Chase, Catherine Tucker, Susan Spicer, Bradley Black, Louis Michot and the Lost Bayou Ramblers, Johanna Divine, Lionel Robin, Dave Robicheaux, the Figs, Mike Tidwell, and Richard McCarthy.

*New Mexico:* Joseph Jaramillo, Shawn Kelley, Matt Romero, Isaura Andaluz, Bill Fleming, Enrique LaMadrid, Estevan Arrellano, Paula García, and Bruce Milne.

*Wisconsin, Illinois, Maryland, and Virginia:* Larry Hussli, MaryAnn Hussli and David Hussli, Dick Zondag and others at Jung Seeds, the Whealy family, Michael Twitty, Peter Hatch, Jackie Coldsmith, Greg and Kris Thorne, Scott Carlson, Lawrence Latane, and Laura Lewis.

Gary wishes to thank Agnese Haury and the staff at the Udall Center for Studies in Public Policy and the Institute of Environment at the University of Arizona for time to "re-tool" in order to learn more about how climate change is affecting agriculture. Gregg Garfin, Diana Liverman, and Mike Crimmins were particularly encouraging. Editors of other publications Blake Edgar, Tracey Ryder, Tom Philpott, Bonnie Azab Powell, and Hope Shand guided him in his ways. In addition, Jake Weltzin, Abe Miller-Rushing, and Teresa Crimmins of the National Phenology Network made available many insights on how climate change is affecting plant behavior.

Kraig wishes to thank Jóse Luna Ruiz, Stephen Brush, Marie Jasienuik, and Paul Gepts for their guidance during his research. Thanks also to UC MEXUS, the UC Davis Department of Plant Sciences, and IIE Fulbright for funding portions of his dissertation, which fed into the creation of this book. Also thanks to Mary Tulwilter, who sent us to Robin's.

Kurt wishes to thank the Devotay staff—Kevin Butler, Dan Knowles,

Lucas Donan, Jeremy Tole, Tony Christner, Sally Risk, Morgan Weiss, Jillianne Kinkade, Andrea Heffernan, Jamie Hrudlik, and Constie Brown—for making it possible for him to take all the time necessary to research and write. And special gratitude to his children, Taylor and Devon, his true sources of sustenance and joy.

# LIST OF RECIPES

# HOT SPOTS: AN INTRODUCTION

**THE WORLD AROUND** us is changing in ways we don't always take time to notice or have the perspective to understand. To even begin to comprehend these changes, we sometimes need to contrive an excuse, a mission, that is, *any old reason* that allows us to break away from our ordinary routines so that we may see the earth with fresh eyes. With this in mind, the three of us—Gary, the ethnobotanist; Kraig, the agro-ecologist; and Kurt, the chef—discussed with one another how best to approach a problem like the effects of climate change on our food system. Together, we considered how we might bring new and different perspectives to the table—including the voices of folks whose points of view have yet to contribute to the discussion. And somewhat auda-ciously, we decided to narrow our focus to a single, albeit iconic, food, as a means to facilitate such a discussion. We were going to listen to farmers and chefs, so that we could hear how they felt climate change was affecting them and their livelihoods.

Yes, that's right, *climate change:* everyone's issue du jour or their favorite straw man. It's a topic with geophysical, ecological, social, and political dimensions, but saying anything precise about it seems difficult and very contentious at best. That is because predictions about climate change—at least at this point in time—are prone to be educated guesses and are therefore fraught with some level of uncertainty. Still, while the details of the degree of change, the rates of change, as well as the when and whys of climate change are still up for debate, the change itself is not.

In order to move the discussion forward, some scientists now prefer to call it global climatic destabilization. In the *New York Times,* journalist Thomas Friedman proposed that we dump the term *global warming* altogether, and replace it with *global weirding.* The injection of the term *weirding* implies increasing uncertainty; it concedes that we are facing the prospect of not only an increasingly warmer planet, but one subject to extreme weather events, with more droughts and deluges than previously expected. We just don't know exactly how it will affect the lives—tangibly and on the ground—of food plants, livestock, and humans in any particular locality at *any* point in time.

The notion that we should "go out and look for climate change" was so huge and amorphous as an idea that we feared we could not say it out loud without someone laughing at us. Yet the three of us, representing three very different livelihoods, decided to dedicate a year of our lives to discerning how accelerated climate change *and* other factors might *already* be affecting the diversity of foods grown on this earth. We were going out to the farm fields and into the kitchens to find out. For if these pressures were diminishing the availability and diversity of certain foodstuffs, there was a very real chance that they could also disrupt the food security of our families, our closest friends, and our neighbors.

As a young student prophetically told Gary, the oldest of the three of us: "Climate change will be *the* fundamental issue which shapes what members of my generation do or don't do for the rest of our lives, perhaps just like civil rights was *the* issue for your generation."

Nevertheless, we sensed that we needed to make such an all-encompassing issue as food and climate change a bit more tangible when talking to our friends, and frankly, for ourselves as well. We needed to refocus the mission, to define the boundaries. Our mission would be based around an iconic food that had a fervent following and distinct regional variation in cuisines and products. Wine? Cheese? Beer? No. It was none of these. We would be going on a pepper pilgrimage to the "hot spots" of our continent—the landscapes where unique chiles are grown and are part of the local cultural fabric. Yes, chile peppers were what we sought and why we traveled so many miles. We had pledged like blood brothers to be gastronauts, explorers on what our friend Blake Edgar called a "spice odyssey."

In truth, our purpose was more nuanced than that: We had set out to explore one symbolic food—the chile pepper in all its myriad forms— and how shifting weather has been affecting the pepper's own destiny and the destinies of those who habitually harvest or cook with chiles. We could have chosen any iconic food to serve as our lens for examining climate change, but we had our own personal reasons for selecting peppers.

Some of those reasons had to do with our backgrounds, our skills, and, of course, our own peculiar taste preferences. For starters, Kurt Michael Friese is the chef and owner of Devotay, a restaurant in Iowa City, Iowa, where he creatively incorporates local and seasonal ingredients into a Spanish-inspired, savory cuisine. Over his years as a chef, Kurt has grown to love the smoky Spanish paprikas and the is-this-one-spicy-or-is-it-not roulette of the padron peppers. He keeps the very fiery ones in his repertoire as well, and is quick with a sly smile when anyone says, "It's never too hot for me!" In his so-called spare time, he also publishes a magazine called *Edible Iowa River Valley*—part of the Edible Communities family—and serves on the board of directors of Slow Food USA. On occasion, he and his wife, Kim, have been known to ramp up their gardening endeavors to try to supply much of their restaurant's own fresh produce from their own soil, harvesting it with their own hands.

Kraig Kraft, the youngest in our trio, spent part of his wild youth in New Mexico, where he developed a penchant for eating all kinds of chile peppers. This predilection grew into a bit of an obsession and then the objective of a PhD dissertation in agroecology. By the time we started this joint project, Kraig had already spent two years of his life doing fieldwork on wild chile diversity, covering thirty thousand miles in Mexico while collecting wild chile populations and evaluating the local spicy fare. The project led him to characterize the probable center of domestication for *Capsicum annuum,* the species of chile peppers that most of humankind habitually eats. Kraig also sought out the best vehicles for chile consumption: *tacos de carne asada* in Sonora, or maybe the blue corn *gorditas* with *chorizo* in Peña de Bernal, no definitely the *salbutes* in Mérida . . . well, it looks like he'll have to keep sampling. While residing in northern California, Kraig looked for ways to communicate agricultural and food issues to the larger public, through writing and photography.

Like Kraig, Gary Paul Nabhan has been a chile junkie for as long as he can remember. Some have wondered whether his addiction to piquant peppers is due to his mother using a legendary Aztec method to wean her babies, although Mrs. Nabhan denies this. Aztec women once dabbed chile powder on their nipples to encourage their toddlers to seek other sources of nourishment. Long after he was weaned but before he dropped out of high school, Gary began hanging out with Latinos in a midwestern cantina where a rather daring domesticated rabbit could be enticed to stand up on its hind legs to nibble on pickled jalapeño peppers. Soon after that, he became the wild-chile-eating champion of Baja, Arizona, and a small-scale food producer by avocation, as well as an ecologist and ethnobotanist by vocation. The two tracks converged when he became hell-bent on discovering just *why* chiles are hot and why many cultures favor fiery foods. To frame it as an evolutionary riddle, he wondered why chiles were the only members of the deadly nightshade family that protect themselves not with toxic alkaloids, but by having "hot" fruit. Along the way, Gary became involved with the ecological restoration and market recovery of traditional foods such as the wild chiltepin, and he spearheaded the designation of the first protected area in the United States that was dedicated to a wild relative of a major food crop.

In fact, all of us have been involved in Renewing America's Food Traditions (RAFT), Slow Food USA, and other grassroots efforts to promote and preserve rare place-based foods. Why? Such foods link together our love of certain tastes with our love of particular places, cultural traditions, and culinary preparations. We don't want any more of our food history and favorite local flavors to slip away, as if they could simply be replaced by some facsimile cheaply grown or made in China or Chile, at the same time homogenizing the regional culinary differences that make travel and discovery such stimulating and pleasurable experiences. To advance this food restoration work, we collectively brought to the table our skills as chefs, ecologists, ethnobotanists, folklorists, oral historians, writers, photographers, activists, eaters, and chile addicts. We hoped to model a collaborative approach to culinary conservation, forming a functional squad of gastronauts that could explore some hot spot to listen and to learn what folks thought about the dynamic relationships among shifting weather, pepper production, and chile-tinged cuisines.

Of course, we could not always be sure which apparent shifts in weather patterns or catastrophic events were tightly linked to long-term climate change. In fact, the tightness of linkages between certain plausible causes and their presumed effects in the climate change arena was being not only scientifically challenged but hotly debated during the very months we began our odyssey. We had begun our fieldwork together just prior to the International Conference on Climate Change held in Copenhagen in the early days of 2010.

Even before we left on our spice odyssey, we knew very well what the prophetic voices like those of Al Gore and Bill McKibben had warned about impending climate change, as well why naysayers like Rush Limbaugh and David Bellamy were skeptical that such changes were truly evident. We were appreciative of how Anna Lappé had been working to alert everyone from iPodded students to TV-watching couch potatoes that "the climate crisis is at the end of your fork" through her proposing a *Diet for a Hot Planet*. But we were also painfully aware that American Farm Bureau Federation President Bob Stallman had come out against climate change legislation, drawing a line in the sand between his membership and activists concerned with the way certain industrial agricultural practices may be aggravating global climate change:

> A line must be drawn between our polite and respect-ful engagement with consumers and how we must aggressively respond to extremists who want to drag agriculture back to the days of 40 acres and a mule . . . At the very time when we need to increase our food production, climate change legislation threatens to slash our ability to do so. The world will continue to depend upon food from the United States. To throttle back our ability to produce food—at a time when the United Nations projects billions of more mouths to feed—is a moral failure.

Who we had *not* heard from in a satisfactory way were the people who stood to lose the most from radically shifting weather patterns, which appeared to be increasing the severity and/or frequency of hurricanes, floods, and droughts, whatever their immediate causes. They were North America's own farmers and foragers, its chefs and cooks—folks from all the walks of life that bring us our daily bread, our daily tortillas, and, of course, our daily salsa. Although the Farm Bureau calls itself the Voice of American Agriculture, we wanted to hear the diver-sity of voices on the land that national organizations often fail to listen to, let alone represent.

Some farmers, we had heard, didn't waste much time debating what the causes or rates of shifting weather patterns were—they were too busy trying to adapt their crops and farming practices to respond to altogether unprecedented conditions. We had a sense that they did not see themselves as potential *victims* of either climate change or govern-ment programs to slow it. Instead they saw themselves as actual *problem solvers,* actively experimenting with ways to mitigate or adapt to chang-ing conditions, just as they have always had to do as farmers.

Nevertheless, many farmers, food distributors, and chefs were willing to admit that they are facing an unprecedented level of uncertainty in their businesses, and some of that uncertainty is directly related to global weirding. Many of them agree with what Kerry Trueman once wrote in the Green Fork blog: "Whatever you want to call it, it's real, so the sooner we stop dithering and start taking meaningful steps to halt climate change, the better our chances of avoiding its most catastrophic consequences."

Those consequences will not merely be *physical* challenges to their making ends meet. As the farmers and fishers who survived Hurricanes Katrina and Rita learned, those disasters had economic, ecological, emotional, social, spiritual, cultural, and culinary dimensions to them as well. Whether they perceived them as being triggered by human-made, natural, or even supernatural causes—or a mix of the three—the farmers, gardeners, and chefs we spoke with were already feeling some effects that were keeping them from doing business as usual. We met them in their fields and kitchens, not to pass judgment on the extent to which they accurately understood the causes of climate change, but to hear their own stories of how they were already grappling with and adapting to the effects of wildly fluctuating weather, water availability, pestilence, and plagues.

It was a fairly simple idea: *to listen.* We wanted to listen firsthand to the seldom-heard voices in our food system, rather than taking what bureaucrats in the USDA or the Farm Bureau were saying as the gospel truth. We wanted to see with our own eyes how farmers, farmworkers, food marketers, and chefs were already responding to variations in rainfall, temperature, the duration of the growing season, and the frequency of hurricanes, tornadoes, hailstorms, and floods, as well as the movements of insects, viruses, and bacteria. All of these factors directly affect our food supply, and, ultimately, our food security and capacity for survival.

We had a hunch that climate change wasn't just *out there*—in the polar ice caps and in receding glaciers—but *in here,* in our food system, in our daily bread as well. Farmers and gardeners are well aware of the signposts pointing to shifting weather patterns, and they are seeing those signposts in the fields, fisheries, and fencerows of our nation; in our community co-ops, cafés, and cultural festivals; in the calories, colors, and chemicals of the food we set on our tables to nourish our families.

Perhaps we were stumbling upon an altogether different approach to climate change than the one taken by scholars, bureaucrats, and politicians. Our view of the dilemmas we are facing was not so much filtered by a particular ideology, nor limited to any discipline, as it was focused on a particular crop and the many human hands and minds that brought it to our tables. Because the diversity of the foodstuffs that humans eat is mind-boggling, it would become impossible to discern any pattern of change if we simply jumped from one food to another—from fish and fowl to fava beans, farina, and fennels. Instead, we chose to stick to chiles and, in particular, to use the somewhat translucent pods of place-based heirloom peppers as the lens through which we would examine a world in change.

So why chiles?

Well, as previously mentioned, the three of us happen to be quite fond of the hot little suckers, but perhaps our predilection for pungency was beside the point. Our professional training had made us well aware of the fact that chile peppers are among the world's most widely used crops, serving prominently and variously as spices, condiments, and vegetables in many cultures and cuisines. Not only that, but chile peppers had already survived several earlier bouts with climate change over the millennia. Archaeologists suggest that indigenous peoples of Mexico have been managing and harvesting, dispersing, and consuming chile peppers under shifting climatic regimes for upward of six thousand years. This places them among the five oldest-known fully domesticated crops in all of the Americas.

Linguists suggest that, fifty-five hundred years ago, domesticated chiles had joined maize, magueys, and squashes in the gardens, songs, and stories of the ancestors of the Zapotec, Mixtec, and other Mesoamerican peoples. Over the last few thousand years, these initial crops of the Americas have had to adapt both to natural changes in the climates of their places of origin as well as to their cultural diffusion and cultivation in altogether different climates and farming systems from the ones they first found in the heartland of their domestication. From Mexico, the seeds of chile peppers were first passed to other Mesoamerican and South American cultures, then to those in the Caribbean.

By comparison, the cultivation of chile pepper in the "Old World" or Eastern Hemisphere has had a relatively short history, barely half a millennium. Chile peppers were unknown to the Old World until Columbus brought them to Iberia in the early 1500s. Soon after Columbus, Portuguese, Jewish, and Arab traders brought them to Africa, the Middle East, and South Asia. Since these relatively recent introductions, the diffusion and adoption of chile peppers in other lands has been rapid, for they are now cultivated and consumed on all six inhabited continents. Indian, Thai, Indonesian, Syrian, and Szechuan cuisines have especially embraced the chile pepper and incorporated its characteristic spice and heat as a main part of their dishes.

The chile has become so intertwined with a number of local cuisines that they have appropriated and developed their own varieties and their own ways of preparing or processing the chiles. Some of these examples include Hungarian paprika, the Aleppo or Halaby pepper, the Spanish piquillo pepper, the Thai pepper, and on and on. Globally, more than twenty-five million metric tons of chile peppers are harvested each year for consumption, with China, Mexico, Turkey, Spain, and the United States currently leading the world in both production and consumption of fresh chile peppers.

Spice, vegetable, condiment, colorant, medicine, pest repellent, preservative, weapon—the chile pepper has taken advantage of the various opportunities to accommodate humankind's different needs and gustatory desires. These diverse needs, and the diverse environments where humans live, have given rise to the innumerable varieties of peppers that populate the global landscape.

And yet, what better place to launch our spice odyssey than in Mexico, the motherland of at least three of the domesticated chile species, where wild chiles not only still grow in the sierras, but are still eaten, and still lauded in indigenous songs, stories, sayings, and other cultural lore?

Of course, it was not simply the survival of these diverse species and varieties of chile peppers that interested us, but the survival of time-tried relationships among crops, cultural communities, and their cuisines. As we were soon to see, the piquancy, pungency, and plurality of chile peppers have somehow become reflected in certain people's identities. Peppers are certainly more than mere food; they are also part digestive catalyst, part medicinal miracle worker, and part spiritual cleanser. Chiles even inspire a certain tribal devotion, so to speak, with cultures as disparate as Mayan and Florida Cracker proudly promoting their native chile pride. Their use in most cuisines has little to do with the calories they offer to a meal, and more to do with pleasure, stimulation, well-being, and excitement.

It's time for us to launch this little adventure, so let's all head out into the hot spots of the Americas to get a taste of what is happening with our changing world.

# CHAPTER ONE

# Finding the Wildness of Chiles in Sonora

**WHEN WE CROSSED** the US–Mexico border into the *estado de Sonora,* we could feel something different in the landscape. It was especially visible along the roadsides, a feeling that was palpable in the dusty air. Less than half an hour south of Nogales, Arizona, we began to see dozens of street vendors on the edge of the highway, hawking their wares. There were fruit stands, ceviche and fish tacos in seafood carts, tin-roofed *barbacoa* huts, and all sorts of garish concrete and soapstone lawn ornaments clumped together. Amid all the run-of-the-mill street food and tourist kitsch, we sensed that we might just discover something truly Sonoran.

Dozens of long strings of dried crimson peppers called *chiles de sarta* hung from the beams of the roadside stands, ready for making moles and enchilada sauces. Hidden among them were "recycled" containers used to harbor smaller but more potent peppers: old Coronita beer bottles and the familiar curvy Coca-Cola silhouette filled with home-made pickled wild green chiltepines. These were what we sought— little incendiary wild chiles, stuffed into old bottles like a chile Molotov cocktail and sold on the street.

They signaled to us that we had come into what the likes of Graham Greene and Carlos Fuentes have described as a truly different country—the Mexican borderlands. They are as distinct from the rest of Mexico as they are from the United States, for the borderlands have their own particular food, folklore, and musical traditions. This is a country where a beef frank wrapped in bacon can become a "Sonoran hot dog"—with jalapeños, refried beans, *crema*, and fiery-hot salsa soaked into a soft-textured roll—and where ballads are sung about rebels and renegades, both those of the past like Pancho Villa and those of the present like the *narcotraficantes* of the Sinaloan drug cartel. It is a place where preservative-laden ketchup is frowned upon, and where freshly mashed salsas are nearly as common as water.

We were after the first and most curious of all the North American chile peppers, the chiltepin—the wild chile pepper of the arid subtropical sierras. It remains one of the true cultural icons of the desert borderlands, a quintessential place-based food, for it is still hand-harvested from the wild. Chiltepines are associated with human behaviors that are considered both sacred and profane. On the one hand, they are deified in an ancient Cora Indian creation story, and relied upon in Yaqui and Opata healing and purification rituals. On the other hand, they remain the favored spice in Sonoran cantinas and cathouses.

As to their own behavior, wild chiltepines are a fickle lot. They camouflage themselves and hide deep beneath the thorny canopies of hackberry bushes and mesquite trees, daring us to come after them and shed some blood. Exasperated, some Sonorans have tried to take them out of the wild and domesticate them. They have tried to cultivate them in drip-irrigated, laser-leveled fields, but they have had little luck taking the wildness out of this chile. In the US Southwest, the great demand among Chicanos for its unique flavor has created a market scarcity of the chiltepin. This has pushed prices up above sixty-five dollars per kilo in *mercados* on both sides of the border.

The difference in flavor and kick between the wild chiltepin and its domesticated brethren is much like the difference between Sonora and the rest of Mexico. Perhaps it is the potency of the desert itself that is expressed in the *terroir* of the chiltepin. Or maybe that potency is because it is truly a food of the *borderland*—*verdaderamente de la frontera*—a place so filled with environmental, political, and mythical juxtapositions that it has fire-forged certain unique characteristics in the Sonoran psyche. A disproportionate number of Mexico's revolutionaries, rebels, presidents, dissidents, and saints have come from *el estado de Sonora,* a state of mind as much as a geographic one. No doubt, they were all eaters of the chiltepin, a food that the inimitable Dr. Andrew Weil once declared to be *psychotropic.* Perhaps in Sonora, you are really not *what* but *where* you eat.

The chiltepin is small but as fierce as the desert sun blazing on a summer day. Compared with other, bigger, but watered-down versions of peppers, it packs a terrific punch of pungency per unit ounce. And yet its fire quickly burns out; you are left with a lingering taste of minerals, the thirsty desert earth itself.

It is remarkable that the chiltepin remains one of few wild foods harvested in North America that grosses well over a million dollars in the international marketplace in a good year, for the chiltepin crop is very vulnerable to the vagaries of a harsh and variable climate. For us, Sonora's stressed-out patches of wild peppers were the perfect place to make our first "landing" of our spice odyssey.

And so we careened off the highway pavement and into the desert's dust, where a dozen roadside stands presented themselves on the edge of a Sonoran farming village named Tacícuri. That term is an ancient Pima Indian word for the wild pig-like peccaries known in the Sonoran Desert as javelina. Yes, there were still plenty of javelina, rattlesnakes, and Gila monsters in these parts, but that was not why we slid to a halt before this makeshift marketplace. It was the stunning sight of those six-foot-long strings of red-hot chile peppers that suggested chiltepines might be hidden nearby.

We piled out of our van (which we had long since christened the Spice Ship) and stood there amazed by all the paraphernalia, guaranteed to dazzle any spice lover. Not only were there dozens of fire-engine-red *sartas* strung with hundreds of long chile peppers, there were bottles and bags and baskets and bins full of other chiles as well: *chiles del arbol,* serrano chiles, jalapeños, and chiltepines. There was enough heat on that roadside to cause a nuclear summer if all of the fiery capsaicinoids in those fruits were ever ground and instantaneously let loose into the desert air.

"We have *arrived,*" Gary said to Kurt, who was on his maiden voyage into the deserts of Sonora. Gary had spent most of his "adulthood" in the Sonoran Desert—if in fact he had ever grown up at all—so he was serving as our host for this leg of our journey. However, Kraig was at the helm, for he had recently surveyed most of Mexico on his own, searching for the origins and domestication of chile peppers. Once out in the desert sun, Kraig took Kurt along to rattle off the local names for certain shapes, colors, and sizes that described particular varieties. As a seasoned chef, Kurt knew many of these variants, but by names somewhat different from those used in Sonora.

"Take one and grind it between your fingers," Kraig demonstrated to Kurt, showing him how the locals put dried chiltepines in their food. "Just don't rub your eyes afterward!" he added.

"And remember to wash your hands *before* you visit the *letrina,*" Gary interjected, with a wry smile and an exaggerated gesture toward a nearby outhouse.

Kurt eyed the two of them with a look that said, *I'm not the rookie you take me for.* He had handled far too many peppers in his twenty years as a chef to be vulnerable to that kind of calamity anymore.

Of course, there was more for us to look at than just chiles: huge bins packed full of pomegranates and quinces; monstrous piles of striped cushaw squashes; and coolers full of local cheeses called *queso asadero* or *queso cocido.* The cornucopia of the desert stood before us in all its ragtag splendor.

At the same time, we noticed something peculiar: We were looking at what remained of last year's chile crop, not any harvest gleaned from this year's production. Chiltepines are only harvested during a four-week-long window that shifts some from autumn to autumn, for the peak in their fruiting is triggered by the timing of the midsummer rains. The vendors made it clear to us that this year's crop was coming in late—if at all—and would certainly be modest in scale. No bounty would suddenly appear here; the vendors were getting by with only the saddest remains of last year's harvest to sell. Normally a brilliant crimson, these dried chiltepines had lost a bit of their luster and their color had faded, as if they were sun-bleached.

Yes, the Sonorans reluctantly conceded, this summer's monsoons had not been as heavy as they had hoped. Hearing the vendors hint that this year's outlook might be dismal, Gary's face began to reflect concern that this might not be the best season to introduce Kurt to the wonders of Sonora's wild foods. He would soon ask some old Sonoran friends just what was going on, and he would get an earful.

After buying chile peppers great and small, all of the gastronauts got back into the Spice Ship, which shortly veered off the main highway and hung a right onto a winding country road that landed on the plaza of the pueblo of San Ignacio. There, an ancient mission still stands tall above the surrounding orchards of quince, pomegranates, figs, and limes. First built in 1687 by Jesuit missionaries, who called Sonora "an altogether blessed country," this very mission of San Ignacio had once hosted a grumpy German priest named Ignaz Pfeffercorn. When his Pima Indian neighbors decided to play a prank on old "Padre Peppercorn," exposing him to a little green chiltepin in the early 1700s, his very first bite immediately convinced him that he had experienced hell itself. Padre Peppercorn wrote the priests in a nearby parish that he had been seduced into sampling a culinary surprise that the others might wish to try only with their eyes wide open:

> A kind of wild pepper which the inhabitants call *chiltipin* is found on many hills. It is a bit more bitingly sharp than the [black pepper], yet it is manna to the American palate, and is used with every dish with which it harmonizes . . . I tried for the first time to still my hunger with such a dish. After the first mouthful the tears started to come. I could not say a word and believed I had hell-fire in my mouth. However, one

becomes accustomed to it after frequent bold victo-
ries so that with time, the dish becomes tolerable and
finally agreeable.

Pfeffercorn did at least recognize that his Pima hosts fondly regarded
the same little green, immature chile fruits—the size of peas or capers—
with exceeding pleasure, not anguishing pain. Without revealing
Pfeffercorn's experience some 250 years prior to the arrival of chef
Kurt Friese in the very same place, Kraig and Gary watched him with
morbid fascination as their sidekick took his first culinary communion
in the land where chiles run wild.

Yes, they immediately noticed the cooling sweat pooling on his brow.
Yes, they recorded a prolonged moment of silence, then an anguished
cough. Yes, indeed, Chef Kurt had been rendered utterly speechless by
his first close encounter with wild chiles on their native turf. The inevitable smile soon followed.

When we stopped to park the Spice Ship on the plaza opposite the
mission, a friend immediately forewarned us that we were wanted in
two places at once. Gary had come down to San Ignacio the week prior
to the group's arrival to alert several families to our group's odyssey, and
all were now awaiting us. It was on that pre-trip that Gary had first
heard about the magnitude of the summer drought and the toll it was
taking on all perennial crops, both wild and cultivated.

One of the ladies-in-waiting was Doña Chata Gallego, a spry, ninety-
one-year-old quince paste maker. Hardly eighty pounds soaking wet,
with thin gray hair neatly trimmed into a style vaguely reminiscent of
a pompadour, Doña Chata was still in control. A week earlier, she had
Gary escort her into her backyard to show him an entire tub full of
mottled, misshapen quince fruit, scarcely half the size that he remembered from the best years. She had picked up one of the smallest fruits
and then thrown it back in the bin, unable to hide her disgust and
frowning like a sad-sack clown.

"What's going on, Doña Chata?" Gary had asked her in Spanish. He
was there to listen, and listen he did.

"It hasn't rained, has *not* rained," she scolded, looking up to the heavens and shaking her bony, crooked finger to the dry cloudless sky. "The quinces are smaller than usual, in fact, tinier than they have *ever* been. The peaches didn't grow either. It has been *so dry* this summer."

Gary's own experience living some sixty miles north of her that summer somewhat corroborated her opinion; his hometown of Patagonia had suffered its driest recorded year since the 1890s. May and June had seemed rather cool and, in fact, had coughed up three or four minor sprinkles, which was something unusual for the end of spring in the desert. But as ranchers in both Arizona and Sonora had long warned him, when little rains come at the end of spring, there is a delay or disruption of the big summer rains—the thunder-and-lightning, gully-washing monsoons that are simply called *las aguas* by Sonorans. Local knowledge appeared right on target this year. Not only did borderlands meteorologists record that July and August of 2009 were as dry as they had been for years, but the meager rains that did arrive came late, as if the storm patterns that offered them up had been delayed.

Arriving at the San Ignacio plaza for the second time in two weeks, Gary first ushered us into the historic adobe home of the Sanchez family, traditional farmers he had first met in 1975. Maria del Carmen, the oldest sister, had prepared a hearty peasant meal of *carne con chile colorado,* refried beans, spiced rice, hand-stretched wheat tortillas, chiltepin salsa, and rice pudding for us.

Meanwhile, Jesús Sanchez, Gary's oldest friend in the village, sat down to eat with us and started to talk about the weather, as it seems farmers everywhere in the world are apt to do, even before other more mundane topics are broached. Jesús had a broad face that had been bronzed by the desert sun, but at age sixty he was as strong as he had been when Gary first encountered him some thirty years ago. Gary asked him to comment on Doña Chata's dire predictions about how prolonged drought would ultimately affect the entire harvest.

Jesús began in a somewhat circumspect manner, not wanting to contradict his elderly neighbor. Nevertheless, he felt that he had to offer a more nuanced perspective: "Well, it's raining now, but when the trees really needed it, there just wasn't enough rain. The fruit are not only smaller, but they have become pockmarked by a hailstorm that arrived in September. The pomegranates were already at a stage of maturation where they got really damaged by the hailstones. They were that big," he added, curling his index finger and clasping it together with his thumb.

He cleared his throat and paused so that we could absorb and translate his words. He spoke in the matter-of-fact tone of someone who has painstakingly observed the effects of lots of different kinds of weather in the same place over many, many years. That's what a desert farmer gets used to doing—facing dramatic swings in the quantity and intensity of precipitation as well as in the severity of heat from year to year. But Jesús modestly hinted that there was something happening here that was (or at least appeared to be) beyond what he had experienced in the past.

His eyebrows rose and twitched as he continued, "The curious thing is *when* the hail came this year. Usually if it hails, it's in August, when the fruit are small and held tight on their stems so that they're hard to damage. We know how to deal with any incidental damage when that happens, pruning the damaged branches back so that the remaining fruit reach larger sizes. Then the entire tree isn't burdened by so many small fruit. But this year, the hailstorm came later, when a lot of fruit were getting big, and we've witnessed them suffering a lot of damage."

Jesús was not directly forecasting the fate of chiles for this particular year, but he was revealing something that wild harvesters as well as farmers would tell us wherever we stopped to talk to them in Sonora: They *expect* the rains to wax and wane from year to year, but they don't quite know what to do when heavy rains, hailstorms, hurricanes, or floods arrive in an untimely manner. *Unseasonal* or *unexpected* is the word farmers use, but they spit it out of their mouths as if they are saying *unnatural*.

In other words, what scientists call *outside of the normal range of variation* spells uncertainty, if not outright trouble, for farmers and foragers, the provisioners of our food security.

But just when we thought Jesús was going to continue, as some farmers often do, in a completely fatalistic rant, he reminded us that climate change is not exactly the bane of every crop. "You know, of course, the climate has been changing all along, but after our father died in 1998, I realized that I could try some fruits that he never would have been able to grow here when he was a younger man. I can now grow different kinds of avocados, as well as some truly tropical fruits like mangoes, guavas, and papayas. For some reason, strawberries grow well here now. We really couldn't successfully grow such fruit crops here up until about eight years ago. It's too bad that my father didn't see them; they would have filled him with wonder . . ."

His father, Casimiro Sanchez Senior, was always delighted by the unexpected. Before he died at the age of ninety-five in 1998, he had been a mentor to Gary and many others for decades, for he was a true storyteller of the life and times of rural Sonora. During the last days of the Mexican Revolution, while he was still just a boy, he had begun farming to feed his mother and siblings after his father had been killed. With astonishing detail, he could cite the years and even the months of the great floods and droughts that had occurred in Sonora over the entire span of the twentieth century. When we asked Jesús, as Casimiro's second son, which of those flood years he personally remembered, his answer surprised us, for it did not follow any script we had heard about climate change.

"Oddly, we're not having big floods here in the Magdalena Valley now as frequently as we did during my father's time on earth. Others may be getting massive floods, but we're not anymore, at least not right here. The last big one to hit this valley was in 1993. Before that, 1989. I remember the previous one well—it was a whopper of a flood that came on the fringe of a hurricane in 1979. Before that, 1969.

"Now, I'm not saying that it's all benign. We may be having fewer floods, fewer hard freezes, a longer growing season. But in some parts around here, especially at the lower margins, the apple trees just don't bear fruit anymore. Some peaches have been negatively affected by the hotter climate as well. We've had to change varieties. We now grow a flat-faced peach—we call it *durazno chato*—that we got from the lowlands over by Baja California."

Gary recalled to Jesús what Arizona's agricultural meteorologist Dr. Paul Brown had told him earlier during a conversation in which Paul had expressed his concern for how shifting weather patterns might be affecting desert fruit crops: "I'm not worried so much about annual crops in the desert lowlands or tree crops in the mountain valleys as I am about perennial crops growing below two thousand feet in elevation."

Paul went on to describe the rise in nighttime temperatures that the Sonoran Desert has already received. "I just don't see how those trees and vines will still get the winter chill hours they need to flower and fruit."

What Dr. Brown suggests holds true not only for Sonora, but for other lowland regions as well. In a recent study, Dr. Eike Luedeling looked at historical temperatures in California's Central Valley—the epicenter of fruit and nut production in the United States, with crops worth more than nine billion dollars annually. He concluded that, by the middle of this century, the valley will no longer have sufficient chilling hours to trigger the flowering and fruit production of its characteristic tree crops. Eike has commented to us that this phenomenon is already decreasing fruit yields in other deserts—such as the one in Oman on the eastern coast of the Arabian Peninsula—not just the Sonoran. The way rising temperatures are reducing chill hours below the critical threshold needed by fruit trees has recently become a phenomenon of global concern.

As Gary translated Brown and Luedeling's conclusions into Spanish, Jesús nodded in agreement. We asked him whether he believed that the drought that began between 1998 and 2000 was finally coming to an end. His answer was terse: "It's still not raining like it normally does."

He looked outside through the window, then continued. "The water table that we tap into with our wells is lower than it's ever been. Even after some rains, it doesn't appear to have recovered much. That's not only because of the effects of the drought. It's also because there's more pumping now, more competition for scarce groundwater.

"But as a farmer, I still see evidence of the prolonged drought. The rains have not yet replenished the moisture in the soil of our fields. Nor have they replenished the groundwater . . ."

Just then the older brother of Jesús, Casimiro Junior, peeked his head out from the kitchen. A skinnier version of Jesús, with high cheekbones and gaunt cheeks, Casimiro sometimes plays the contrarian in the family. Most of the time now, he lives alone in the orchard under a sprawling *ramada* rather than coming up to the home in the village that has been in his family for nearly a century. He tipped his baseball cap to everyone, then motioned toward the door.

"I don't think you came here just to sit like squash on a shelf, I thought you wanted to go and see some of my chiles in the field, or learn how our sister cooks them up in this kitchen. Come on into the kitchen for a little bit so Maria del Carmen can show you how to make her salsa, then I will take you over to our orchard. You need to walk off some of that food you've just eaten . . ." He rubbed his belly, then pointed to Gary's ample torso.

Kraig and Kurt crowded into the tiny kitchen with Maria del Carmen and her sister. In the corner was a wood-burning stove, that is, an oven shaped from adobes topped by two "burners"—holes above the coals that were suitable for setting cookware on. One burner was topped with a flat piece of smoke-blackened steel with a small handle— a *comal* to cook and warm tortillas. On the other sat a charred and juice-stained stockpot full of bubbling beans. On the opposite side of the door from the woodstove sat a four-burner propane-fueled modern range. The range harbored a couple of small saucepans, one of which held the *chile colorado* that had so delighted the gastronauts when they sat at the dining table just a few minutes before.

"How do you make that sauce?" Kurt asked. Kraig stepped in to translate as Maria del Carmen began to describe her time-tested process of making *chile colorado*.

"First, the meat is simmered with garlic, oregano, and salt. The sauce is made from the dried chiles from the *sarta*. We boil the chiles with water for twenty minutes or so, then we brown some flour with oil, and then whip the softened chiles in a blender. We add this to the browned flour and then add the shredded meat." She pulled a strand of hair back from her face and shyly smiled. "It's simple," she added, as if she had been making *chile colorado* for a long time without anyone ever having asked her how she did it.

Kraig translated this into English as Kurt peered into the pots and nodded.

When it came to learning about the *salsa de chiltepin* we had been served, we were surprised to hear from Casimiro and Maria del Carmen that they hadn't really used the local, wild chile of Sonoran tradition to make the salsa that day. Instead, Maria del Carmen had used a similar but cultivated perennial chile grown in the understory of Casimiro's orchard crops. While almost everyone in the region preferred truly wild chiltepines over other peppers in their salsas, the great demand and smallish crops had raised their prices a bit too high for folks of modest means.

"I have a couple of those plants growing here in our dooryard garden," Casimiro explained, "but let's hop into your vehicle, and I'll show you how many we have growing in the orchard."

Guided by both Casimiro and Jesús, we meandered down dusty lanes lined with fruit trees, dropping off the mesa where the mission was built, and down onto the floodplain of the Rio Magdalena. This time, when we piled out of the Spice Ship, we were led through a gate into a world that was lush, cool, and shady. While the prolonged drought continues to have an impact on both cattle and wild chile production in the surrounding desert canyons, here was a refuge from the heat and aridity, a sanctuary of shade and luscious fruit nourished by waters running down a 350-year-old irrigation ditch.

Jesús stuck his hand into the clear running waters, splashed them onto his face, and gestured to the ancient stone-lined trough through which they ran.

"This acequia is older than the historic mission buildings up in the pueblo," he reminded us. "It's been irrigating quince, pomegranate, and fig trees since the Spanish first arrived and planted them here. But now it's also watering a number of other fruits we're trying to grow because of the changing climate: avocados, guavas, pumelos, flat-faced peaches, limes, lemons, mangoes, and persimmons."

As we strolled along under the overlapping canopies of so many fruit trees, Kraig spotted a patch of some perennial chiles growing deep in their shade. Jesús signaled Kraig to come over and take a good look at them. The woody perennial peppers appeared to be one and a half to three years old; most were thigh-high, but the oldest ones reached up to our chests. Casimiro picked some slightly beaked green and red fruit off one of the plants and handed them to Gary. Gary passed them over to Kraig, asking, "Are these some other kind of bird pepper?"

Kraig carefully looked them over. "Well, these are pretty close in appearance to the wild chiltepines found locally, but take another look: The fruit are too pointed to be true chiltepines. Folks all throughout Mexico keep a couple of plants of this pepper; they are feral chiles—sort of mongrel mixes of wild and domestic varieties. You'll see them in patio gardens or in orchards."

Kraig picked a handful and took a close look at them. "They are all really similar and have certain of the same characteristics—small size, oval fruit, waxy small leaves . . . The birds love them and disperse them all over the place. These make a nice substitute because no one has any real luck growing the wild chile. If you put the chiltepin in an agricultural setting, you must coddle it—it just doesn't like to get its roots too wet . . . it's too susceptible to picking up all sorts of diseases."

Even with his limited English, Casimiro had picked up that we were debating the differences among truly wild and semi-cultivated chiles.

"Look how many of these chiles we're getting in such a small space. Of course, they don't sell for as much as the truly wild *chiltepines del monte,* but they're easier to pick. The wild chiltepines are scattered beneath hackberries and mesquite, and sometimes hard to find.

"You might see one over there." Casimiro signaled toward the orchard's edge some thirty yards away. "But the next one might be far away, way over in that direction," he said, pointing to the gate through which we had come. "So that's why this *chile pequin del jardin* sells for only 100 to 120 pesos per kilo, while the true *chiltepin del monte* sells for as much as 500 to 600. And when the drought makes them scarce, sometimes they even go for more," Casimiro concluded.

As we had heard from our colleague Kimberlee Chambers, who was off surveying the 2009 chiltepin crop some hundred miles to the east of San Ignacio, the drought in northern Sonora was indeed pushing up prices for truly wild chiles. The drought's effects were not limited to the paucity of moisture diminishing the production of fruit. Compared with other years, there were also more moth larvae infesting the fruit. In the worst years, these little *gusanos* infest as much as half the chile fruit in certain wild populations, eating the seeds inside and, for the most part, spoiling the value of the chiltepines. But here in the shade of quince and peach, the moths could hardly find the perennial chiles, which were well watered, naturally fertilized, and apparently resistant to insect attack. We saw no evidence of their larvae making holes in the green or the red fruit.

We said good-bye to Casimiro, and while Jesús was accompanying us over to Doña Chata's to taste another version of *salsa de chiltepin,* we discussed how two things were becoming glaringly apparent. First, the ways that wild desert foods like the *chiltepin del monte* respond to shifting weather are different from those of cultivated food crops like the *chile pequin del jardin,* as it sits with its toes in the water and its head in the cool shade. Both kinds of foods may be essential to local food security, but they have altogether different vulnerabilities, so that, even at the same site, one may be more affected than the other.

Second, as global or regional weather patterns shift, it seemed to us that each location would have its own unique manifestations of those shifts. We began to wonder whether any two places might respond the same way.

In the face of such unpredictability, what's a farmer to do? Fred Kirschenmann, a Dakota grain farmer associated with the Stone Barns Center for Sustainable Agriculture, has pondered this dilemma for some time. The answer that Fred has come up with seems to be generally in line with what Casimiro and Jesús are already doing: "The only thing that the experts can agree on that they think will bear out during our lifetimes is that we will have more unstable climates. And one of the few ways that we as farmers can gain resilience in our food system—that is, to buffer ourselves from climate change—is by having more diversity in our fields and orchards."

There in the dooryard garden of Doña Chata, just as in the flood-plain orchard of Casimiro and Jesús, we felt that diversity of food crops cooling us, shading us, nourishing us, and filling our nostrils with heav-enly fragrances. That diversity was not merely good for our eyes and our noses to behold; it was good to eat, and good for buffering us against the unknown.

We hugged Doña Chata and Jesús, then went on our way, down to the Feast of Saint Francis celebration in Magdalena, Sonora, and beyond. Already we had formulated a new objective: to see just how uniform or heterogeneous the effects of shifting weather were on food production within the very same valley, and across valleys in the same Sonoran Desert landscape. Did other farmers and foragers tell stories radically different from those of Casimiro and Jesús about how changes in climatic patterns might be affecting their chile harvests?

The road south from Magdalena, Sonora, led into climes that are typi-cally hotter and drier than those we had experienced in San Ignacio. But the plains region of the Sonoran Desert had already been suffering drought for most of the last nine years, and this year seemed to be no exception. Kraig and Gary had already received a number of reports suggesting that the wild chiltepin harvest in most localities north of Sonora's capital, Hermosillo, would be the worst in years.

And yet we had also been alerted to an extraordinary event that had happened just a month before our visit on the coastal plains south of Hermosillo, where the Sonoran Desert meets the subtropical thornscrub northeast of the Gulf of California port of Guaymas. The remnants of Hurricane Jimena had arrived just north of the Guaymas region during the first week of September and had dumped an ungodly amount of rain on the plains in a matter of thirty-six hours.

We beelined toward the port town of Guaymas, with only a brief stop in Hermosillo for fish tacos, roasted *chile güero* salsa (soaked in lime juice and Worcestershire sauce), and a short chat with desert ecologists Alberto Búrquez and Gela Martinez. We asked them about damage from the recent hurricane.

"You just won't believe it." Alberto sighed, shaking his head. He was Sonoran-born but internationally renowned for his studies of environmental change in desert and tropical ecosystems. He ran his hand back through his slightly graying hair, perhaps as a way to sound more objective while he recounted the chaos that he had witnessed less than a month earlier.

"Bridges collapsed, and the highway pavement on either side of them was completely washed away. In just twenty-four hours, they received somewhere between 700 and 730 millimeters [twenty-seven to twenty-eight inches] of rain. That's two and a half times their average *annual* precipitation arriving in *just one day*. The rain streamed down the slopes of the inland mountains, and then the flood roared across the coastal plains two to three meters deep, literally pushing the ocean waters back when it flowed across the beaches . . ."

This did not sound like a tropical storm that had confined itself to the normal range of variation. It had broken all records in the state of Sonora for the amount of rain heaped onto these otherwise dry lands by a single hurricane. What Alberto told us begged the question: Could such an extraordinary storm be linked in any way to the working hypothesis of global climate change?

Well, it was hard to say, but most scientists would beg off from saying that any *single* event indicates anything. As much as the media would like to put some spin on enormously destructive events like Hurricanes Katrina, Mitch, or Jimena, one showstopping hurricane in isolation cannot be used as an indication of unidirectional changes in weather patterns. At the same time, meteorologists have been able to confirm that, in general, the frequency and ferocity of such hurricanes have been increasing with the current rates of global warming. One recent analysis of weather records has suggested that hurricane frequencies have doubled over the last two decades. Climatologists have amply documented that today's hurricanes have become far more intense, with faster wind speeds and heavier rains as they reach their peak velocities.

Alberto's wife, Gela, had something to say about all this. Her lovely head of curls rained down upon her suntanned shoulders as she talked. Because her technical studies delved into issues of leaf litter decomposition and nutrient release, it was not surprising that she had been keen on recording what the storm had left behind. Gela had been stunned by all the flotsam and jetsam that she and her family had seen on the beaches of the Gulf of California immediately after the storm: "Millions of cans and bottles and bags mixed with seaweeds and sponges and even slippers and shoes, all piled in huge mounds that were strewn all the way down the beaches."

As we devoured the last of our fish tacos, Alberto detailed exactly where we should go to witness how the hurricane had potentially affected farmers and chile harvesters.

"They're already fixing up the highways and the bridges so you should be able to get through, but I have no idea how bad it still may be once you get back on the farms. So just be careful how you drive. There is mud everywhere."

The Spice Ship was sailing out on the highway to Guaymas within fifteen minutes of leaving Tito's Mariscos, fully loaded on fish tacos and roasted *chile güero* salsa. Once we passed Hermosillo's southern edge, we began looking for the first telltale signs of floods along the roadside. Curiously, Hermosillo had received barely a sprinkle when the hurricane landed in Sonora, and the same looked true for most of the landscape on the way down into Guaymas.

But then, just past the ancient junction of Los Arrieros—perhaps fifteen miles from the Guaymas city limits—the vegetation began to change in color, texture, and density. In particular, we scanned the landscape for "streamside" vegetation that typically concealed chiltepines beneath hackberry trees along the banks of dry washes.

But the washes weren't dry anymore. They were pockmarked with small puddles and tons of new sprouts of the insidiously invasive weed called buffelgrass. The little vegetation that was left along the arroyo clung precariously to its banks, with many tree roots exposed by recent erosion. It appeared that just a few weeks before, torrents had run through the culverts under the highway as if they were hardly more than funnels; once on the coastal side of the highway, the floodwaters had jumped their channels and spread out clear across the landscape. The buffelgrass was vivid green and spreading its seeds to the wind, and the wild native amaranths were tall and rangy. Above them, all the desert trees looked beat-up, as if they had been pummeled by raging winds.

"Look over there." Kraig pointed ahead, across the median. "We're going down to one lane; the other side of highway has been completely washed out, and its trucks are detouring over here."

"Holy *mole!*" Gary exclaimed. "Look up there—the entire overpass must have collapsed, or was washed away." The passengers groaned and held on as we dipped off the elevated roadbed and down onto a make-shift lane in the median.

When we came back up onto the pavement again, we looked out over the landscape and realized that we must have arrived near Ground Zero of the most massive flood to hit Sonora in many years. Power lines were tilted, trees were uprooted, churned-up mud and standing water were everywhere. Our chances of finding any chiltepines left nearby were slim to none. And yet there might be the possibility of finding farmers nearby who had weathered the storm.

Once we arrived at the cloverleaf intersection between the highways to Guaymas and Bahia San Carlos and those to Navajoa and points south, we began looking inland, hoping to spot a farmstead or orchard that still appeared to be accessible. Gary fixed his sights on some euca-lyptus trees back in the midst of a citrus plantation, drove the van off the elevated roadbed once again, and plunged through a series of puddles as large and as deep as a toddler's swimming pool. We turned a corner when we arrived at the first orange trees and came to a stop in front of a barnyard thick with mud and littered with swamped vehicles. When we got out of the van, the first thing we noticed was that we were surrounded by dragonflies.

*Dragonflies?* They're not exactly commonplace in deserts or even in the dry subtropics, yet there they were, fairly swarming all around us. The noise of the Spice Ship splashing through puddles must have brought the remaining residents out of their midday siesta. One older man in a white cowboy hat looked up at us briefly, then went back to work on a piece of machinery. Another, younger man—really, a mountain of a man, huge and swarthy by comparison with his elderly relative—lurched out of a mud-stained adobe farmhouse and waved. He then took a swig from a liter bottle of beer, set it down on a pile of debris, and waddled over through the mud to greet us.

Sergio Araújo was his name. He was tall, stocky like an offensive lineman, and his broad head was covered with a mass of curly brown hair that verged on being an Afro. He told us that he typically tended eight hectares of orchards—about twenty acres—but he wasn't sure anymore how much of that area would still produce a fruit crop.

We looked at him. There was no way we could be certain that his countenance had changed since the hurricane, but it seemed that he was suffering some kind of post-traumatic stress. His eyes were oddly sucked back into their sockets, almost hidden by the fleshiness of his face, while his lips protruded as if pursed into a permanent frown. It was clear that he had a headache—though whether from the beer or from dealing with the aftermath wasn't so clear.

"How did it look through here when *Huracán Jimena* landed?" one of us asked.

He started to speak, paused, and then slowly raised his beefy hand up, up, up, until it was nearly at the height of his collarbone.

"When the water ran through here, it was more than two meters deep, even two and a half in some places. I'm not kidding you—you can see for yourself. Look at the debris caught up there in the branches, and over there, all that trash perched up in the canopy. So it must have knocked off about 20 percent of all the developing fruit in the entire orchard. Just knocked them down, washed most of them away."

He paused again, as if catching his breath and trying to slow a heart that had been beating under a great deal of pressure for the last month.

"But look, just *look* at the rest . . ."

He slowly turned and stretched his hand out toward the closest row of citrus trees. The skins of the oranges were typically a bright, solid green at this time of the year, but all the fruit that we saw were mottled, pocked, or stained with sickly yellow and black.

"By harvest time, the skins must be ripened to a uniform color, but I don't know how that will happen this year. Once they are scrutinized, I doubt whether the buyers will take *any* of them . . ."

Silence. Sergio's mouth shut in its deeply set frown.

"Well, where did the water come from?" Gary asked.

Sergio finally laughed a little. "It came from *every*where. There wasn't even an arroyo here before. Sometime during the thirty-six hours of rain, the watercourse moved over this way. It's usually dry and was about a kilometer and a half away. Now the channel is within five hundred meters of my house here. But it didn't just run in the channel, it ran all around us, right through the orchard. It took out a quarter hectare of orange trees, ruined every motor and pump we've ever used, damaged everything left on the floors of our buildings, and toppled a twenty-meter eucalyptus tree along our entranceway. It was good you drove in the back way, parked, and climbed through the fence. Otherwise you wouldn't have gotten in here."

"Have any government people gotten over here to help you?" Gary asked.

Kraig stepped in, trying to phrase the question another way in Spanish. "It seems that the government is already taking care of the highway in front of your place, and clearing away debris so it can rebuild the bridges. Has it offered assistance? Before, during, or after the *tormenta*?"

This time, Sergio Araújo almost sneered, but he held back his contempt and tried to turn the whole ordeal into a sad joke. "You aren't going to believe this, but we had no notice that we were going to be hit. No word of any kind reached us in time. And we haven't seen anyone from the government since, except for those road construction workers out on the highway.

"Well, maybe I'm not exactly remembering everything. We must have heard from the teachers not to bring my daughter back to school for the first three weeks. Trees had fallen on the small concrete-block building where she had taken her classes before. They're trying to clean it up, and they just reopened the school this week in another building . . ."

"So how long do you think it will take for your production to recover?" Kraig asked.

"Well, this season we expect to pick just 120 to 140 tons of oranges instead of the typical 200. No, let me see if I'm figuring that right. We totally lost a quarter hectare of mature trees, so no fruit there. Then, instead of 25 to 30 tons per hectare I've been getting on the rest, I may get 8 to 10 tons each. Does that add up? No, it doesn't. Anyway, the skins are all damaged, so the fruit we haven't yet lost will still fetch a lower price, if we can sell them at all . . ."

At this point, Sergio seemed confused and started to breathe heavily, as if his huge body had suddenly run out of air. We let him breathe for a while, and watched the dragonflies hovering over him.

"I don't think I answered your question," he said quietly, once he had recovered. "Pretty soon, we have to walk through the orchard and clear out the broken branches to assess what's left. If we then prune the trees back and level the ground again, it may take two or three more years after that for them to fully recover. Maybe then we can get back to normal . . ."

We thanked him for his answers and departed from the farmyard, for it was time to just let him be. Perhaps shared among all of us was the sinking feeling that neither Sergio's orchard nor anyone else's might ever get back to what we used to know as *normal*.

Before getting back into the Spice Ship, we walked over to the back of Sergio's citrus orchard, to see just how close to his trees the watercourse had shifted. Just beyond his fence, built to keep out cows, the former arroyo was now a broad riverbed filled with a half-mile length of standing water. Egrets and herons waded knee-deep in water where a cactus-studded desert had been just weeks before. And, of course, the instantaneous oasis was swarming with dragonflies.

What surprised us was just how narrow the swath of the hurricane was. It appeared that when *Huracán Jimena* hit the Sonoran coast, the damage done by its winds and floods was hardly twenty-four miles wide. And we struggled for a while, driving around in circles on the few still-functional paved roads, hoping to determine whether Sergio Araújo's crop losses were unique—a data set of one—or whether other farmers and foragers were affected as well.

When we found the mixed citrus grove a mile or so away from Sergio's farm, and heard Oscar González and his young helper Chano recount their tragedy, we became convinced that our larger narrative could not limit itself to chiles alone. Wild chiles no doubt grew in the area before the storm, but they may have been ripped out of the ground by floods, or buried under mud. And yet the fate of perennial fruit crops such as citrus provided a telling contrast with that of widely scattered wild chiles. The more infrastructure you develop as a farmer to pamper your tree crops, the more you risk losing it when catastrophic winds, floods, or fires descend upon your land. In contrast, new wild chile seeds germinate, old ones become unburied, and, with no overhead costs to bear, the life of the pepper burns on.

As we drove up to this second citrus grove, we spotted the young farmworker Chano toiling alone. He was trying to mend fences in order to keep neighbors' cattle out of the orchard plantings, so that they would not do further damage to drip irrigation lines as well as trees. But when we tried to talk to him about the flood, his post-traumatic stress surfaced even more quickly than Sergio Araújo's had done. He pointed to a tall palo verde tree across the way and brushed us off, simply saying, "Go find Oscar González over there and he'll tell you about the tree." It made no sense to us, but still we followed his advice and moved on.

We came into a yard where a brand-new diesel pickup truck had its doors wide open so that everything within it could dry out. We parked next to it and knocked on the door of a neat cabin. After a couple of minutes, Oscar González appeared shirtless and shoeless at the door, a sixty-nine-year-old man who had lost most of his hair but none of his humanity. He apologized that his wife did not immediately come out to greet us, explaining that she had been ill and was resting, but he would be sure to introduce her to us before we left.

Oscar wore nothing but shorts. His chest and back displayed massive scars from accidents and operations, but there was still something *intact* if not exactly elegant about Oscar.

When we asked about the status of the orchard, he immediately assumed that we had come to his home in some official capacity. He politely deferred us to his brother-in-law in the city—the actual owner of the grove—as the one who should be spoken to.

We looked at one another. We didn't exactly look like bureaucrats.

"No, no," Kraig explained in Spanish, "we're not from the government. We're involved in food and agriculture work, but we're here on our own, not representing any agency. We simply want to know what happened to your crop, and what happened to you and to Chano . . ."

He looked at us again, and seemed to sense that we were simply other individuals on this earth, nothing more, nothing less.

"Come, I'll show you."

Without even putting any shoes on—they had probably washed away and been piled up on some beach miles away—Oscar took off through the citrus grove, hobbling and shuffling along in his bare feet.

"Look there, the floodwaters toppled various trees. Look right where that one fell, those aluminum irrigation pipes are now filled with sand, while others have completely washed away from the farm. The drip irrigation lines, look over here. It's not only partially buried, but that one segment there is cut, probably by the hooves of cattle. The fences are all down, every one of them, so the cows come in from all over. That's why Chano is working on the fences first.

"I've counted some twenty trees so far that have fallen over, and I'd like to see if I can prop them up, but I can't do a thing until I get that tractor fixed over there. Two meters of water washed over it, so the engine got swamped, the gas tank filled with water, the alternator and starter wires are ruined, the filters are all clogged with mud. I'm not kidding you, the water was against every tree trunk up to here . . ." He showed us the watermark on the tree trunk in front of him.

"Even for the trees that remain standing, their fruits were hit hard. I'd guess that nearly half of them are stained, spotted, or pocked with rot. And look at how much of them are already down on the muddy ground already, blotched or blackened, rotting away."

He waved to the downed trees as if he were telling them, *To hell with you for the moment, I'll take care of you a bit later,* and then he limped over to his well in the ground and a holding tank above ground level.

"Even if I scrape together enough money from me and my brother-in-law to fix the tractor, I just don't know yet what I'm going to do with the well. Come over here with me and look at this up close. The pumping apparatus slipped down into the shaft and is completely covered with all the sand that flowed into the well during the height of the flood. All this sand that has capped the aquifer has made it so it is inaccessible. The only reachable water is sitting on top of the sand, and it is reddish brown wastewater, completely filthy, that poured across our land from who knows where? Dumps? Animal pens?"

Oscar's sight darted from one problem to another. "See these wires to the power source? They are damp to the touch, still all wet, we'll probably have to replace them. The fuse box, too. I have no idea yet how much all this is going to cost. We put it in over the last fifteen years . . ."

As Oscar's anxiety grew, he began to jolt with pain emanating from his neck and his upper back. And he began to limp more laboriously as well, since some of the pangs of pain ran all the way down his leg to his ankle. However, he kept walking, mumbling that he wanted to show us just two more things.

"See this concrete foundation here? That was where we had a house for our farmworker, Chano. And now Chano's house is completely gone. It collapsed under the weight of the rain. Then most of it was hauled away by the floods, the current was so strong.

"He had called me over this way to help him save it or some of the things inside. But we couldn't. So we went over toward where the chicken coop was getting washed away as well . . ."

Oscar abruptly turned and walked over to a twenty-foot-tall palo verde tree that had served as the axis around which a wire-mesh chicken coop had once been built.

"You could hear the sound of floodwaters gurgling, groaning to uplift one thing after another. The chicken wire came loose and the hens washed away. Chano and I waded over to deal with it, but then realized we couldn't get back to the house. The palo verde tree grew out of a mound that offered slightly higher ground, but soon we had to crawl up into its branches to escape the rising waters."

He gestured toward the higher branches of what looked to us like a spindly, insubstantial little tree.

Then Oscar broke down and began to weep.

"The two of us, Chano and me, we just hung on for dear life. Hour after hour. Maybe three, probably four hours. We watched the flood carry away our farm—even one of the dogs was carried away. Because of the back accident that had brought me back home to Mexico, the pain was intolerable. I could hardly stand staying in one position any longer. Stuck in a tree, holding on, unable to move."

He could not help but cry. He stopped talking for a while and simply wept. We all stood there silent, listening to the breeze move through the citrus trees. Soon Oscar began again.

"But we survived, by a miracle from God. I kept on praying to a saint that my daughter in Anaheim, California, had introduced to me. I think that unlikely saint somehow brought us some help from God. Neither of us would be here otherwise. Our survival doesn't make logical sense." He took a breath. Nobody moved.

"After the waters began to drain down, some neighbors found us. They brought us a tank of clean water to drink. Even the dog that was washed away came trotting back after two days. For several more days, we had only some ham that Chano had sequestered away, and a couple dozen tortillas that I had gotten just before the storm. But we had no lights. No refrigeration, nothing. Somehow, people thought to look for us and help us. They helped us survive.

"You know, it was strange. We had heard about a big hurricane off Baja California several days before, and that it might come our way. But the very day before it really hit this coast, all the electricity around here went out. No radio, no TV. No way of knowing what had happened to the storm. But then, in the middle of the night, we heard the rain begin to come. When I woke up and listened, I heard the floodwaters barking, bleating like frogs."

We slowly walked back to Oscar's cabin, where his wife appeared and greeted us. She had been in California during the storm and had only recently returned to Guaymas. The Gonzalezes had spent hours cleaning mud off the floors and walls of the rooms in the cabin, and she showed us the watermarks remaining in their bedroom.

Oscar and Chano, just like Sergio, somehow survived a storm of unprecedented magnitude, one that swept away much of the fruits of their labors and their technological infrastructure as well. All told, *Huracán Jimena* had brought more than thirty-seven million dollars' damage to Mexico, with about a thousand acres of citrus a total loss. But just a few miles south of the destruction, the eight sacred pueblos of the Yaqui Indian Nation received only four inches of rain from the same storm, which was easily enough to pull the wild chiles on their lands out of a decade-long drought. The same hurricane that had gouged a twenty-four-mile-wide path along the central Sonoran coast had revived the ancient tradition of wild chile harvesting by the Yaqui people who call themselves Yoemem.

In essence, the season's wild weather had divided Sonora's chiltepin harvest this year into three parts: the northern populations, which still suffered from prolonged drought and too many *gusanos* infesting the fruit; the central swath near Guaymas, where wild plants were washed away or made inaccessible by mud and collapsed roads; and the southern reaches, which had received enough rainfall to ensure an ample harvest. We had seen no chiltepines near Guaymas, but we had witnessed the undeniable effects of global climatic instability. After giving Oscar's wife some money for medicine to treat the old man's back pain, we drove south from Guaymas in time to reach the Yaqui villages just after sundown.

Southern Sonora is the land of the Yaqui (Yoemem) and their close relatives, the Mayo (Yoremem). We had some rather whimsical reasons for wanting to talk with them, but none of them had to do with the so-called Yaqui Way of Knowledge made infamous by Carlos Casteneda's best-selling novels. Our quest was much simpler. We wanted to visit the only pueblo in Sonora named for chiltepines: Cocorít, whose name derives from a Yaqui word meaning "place of the piquant *chile del monte*." It appears that Cabeza de Vaca, Estevanico el Moro, and other early Spanish explorers had gone through Cocorít more than four hundred years before our own journey there, recording a flood perhaps as powerful as the one we witnessed, so the town and trails that surround it have considerable antiquity.

We also knew from our readings that, whenever times were tough, the Yaqui and Mayo had survived on their harvests of wild foods. An oral history from 1946 has revealed how a young Yaqui man, Rosalio Moisés, and his recently arrived Mayo bride, Pancha Valenzuela Castro Wailika, survived a time of hunger by working as wild food foragers in the vicinity of Cocorít:

> We walked out in the brush [*monte*] looking for wild food. We did everything we could think of to find food, and indeed we were not often hungry. *Chiltipiquín* grew wild all through the brush, and we would pick a sackful and sell it to the Mexican storekeeper in Vicam; he paid five pesos a kilo. We could pick two or three kilos of chiltipiquíns a week.

We hoped that we would find some elder who had survived that era who would be willing to compare the wild chile harvest of today with the one during the time that Rosalio and Pancha worked as wild foragers. Fortunately, after we spent a night on cots under open-air *ramadas* at a Yaqui *ranchería* at Torim, a bright young Yaqui woman named Anabel suggested that we go to talk to Angel Cota, an elder who had been born in Torim but now lived in Cocorít.

As we tried to locate just exactly where Angel lived in Cocorít, we came upon plenty of evidence that the wild chile harvest there had been substantial. People were selling green chiltepines at the Cocorít farmer's market under the shade of an enormous kapok tree; they were selling them out of their kitchen windows, and hitchhiking into the nearest city, Ciudad Obregon, to sell them there. It appeared that the rains from *Huracán Jimena* had come just in time to stimulate production rather than to disrupt it.

At last we found Angel's daughter, who agreed that her father would be good to talk to about the wild harvest of *co'okoi*, but unfortunately he had been back in the *monte* at their goat ranch and she was not sure when he would return.

Just then, an elderly man in a white cowboy hat came into the backyard. The daughter turned and said, "My father's come back! You're in luck!" He had penetrating eyes, an unshaven face, an unbuttoned cowboy shirt, and a big handshake for us.

He asked us to sit down with him outside in their garden. We told him that we had been buying chiltepines from others in Cocorít, and it looked like it would be a good harvest.

He agreed. There had been less rain the last few years, but this last month they had received enough to make the harvesting of chiltepines lucrative.

"So will everyone be going out to harvest them commercially?" Kraig asked.

"No, not all people here pick their own chiltepines anymore. They'll all have them on their kitchen tables, but those are ones that are gifts or purchases from friends. It's not like in the old days, when I was a youth. It was everyone's seasonal income back then to pick both wild oregano and wild chiles. We'd take them into the market at Ciudad Obregon, or a few buyers would come around. We didn't have many other options for income back then."

"Is Cocorít a good collecting area?" Gary asked.

He smiled. "What do you mean, because of its name? Well, there are a few bushes of wild chiles nearby in the washes, but the harvesters go back into the sierras where they are much denser, near Rancho Corohuisi, Rancho del Mezquite, Rancho Chichiquelite, Rancho de Guayacan . . .

"It seems you are curious about the name of our village. Its full name when it was founded in 1617 was Espiritu Santo de Cocorít, en la Loma de Guamuchíl. Yes, it refers to place of the wild chiles, but in those times, they were referring to the fierceness of the Yaqui people, not just that of the little fruits. Like the hottest chiles, the Yoemem back then were *muy brava, muy fuerte . . . eran valiente, eran matones!*"

What Angel was expressing in Spanish was a sentiment well known throughout Mexico and the Southwest. The Yaqui are considered to be a tenacious, persistent people, one that has kept much of its indigenous culture intact, one that has shown resilience and resistance to detrimental social, economic, and environmental change. When Mexico, much like the United States, subjugated the indigenous groups within its borders through force, the Yaqui were the only ones not to be conquered. Like the wild chiles that survive droughts and floods, the Yaqui are survivors. They are fierce, they are strong, they are courageous, and, when they need to be, they are tough sons of a gun!

Angel Cotam left us with much to think about. We all know that change is inevitable, and that droughts, hurricanes, and floods have wreaked havoc with farmers, foragers, and their food crops for centuries. However, some experts suggest that the rate of climate change has been accelerating. But just what kind or level of change is tolerable, and when should it be considered detrimental? How do people adapt to rapid change? Can they develop enough resilience so that they can resist or at least quickly recover from the worst of climate change, and be opportunistic about reaping the benefits of its windfalls?

Perhaps what Yaqui elder Angel Cotam was suggesting was that plants play an allegorical role in our cultures . . . we emulate their strategies for survival, and use them as symbols to guide us through uncertain

# Chiltepin

*(Capsicum annuum var. glabriusculum)*

It is one of the icons of the desert borderlands, a true place-based food. The chiltepin carves out an existence in a very harsh environment, with limited resources, and does so with the assistance of other organisms. Its incipient existence is dependent on a long chain of ecological interactions. A bird that just gorged itself on a ripe chiltepin fruit perches in a shady spot—an ideal location for a future chiltepin—perhaps in the dense shade of a mesquite or a hackberry tree, where protection from the sun and the deep roots of the tree will help the developing seedling conserve valuable moisture. The bird alights, leaving behind some undigested seeds in its droppings. If everything goes as planned, when the winter rains come, the seeds will germinate. During the spring, the chiltepin plants continue their patient growth hidden in the underbrush, utilizing the precious moisture conserved by the deep roots; then the summer monsoon rains feed their flowering and fruiting cycle. In the fall, the small, globular fruits are raised upward to the sun like an offering and begin to ripen, lighting up the tans and browns of the desert palette with brilliant bursts of crimson and scarlet.

In areas where chiltepines have been harvested and sold, all activity ceases during the harvest season. Local *maquinarias* are often without their workforce as everyone goes into the field to harvest. With retail prices close to sixty dollars per kilo, there are potential windfalls to be had for those who gather up the wild chile. Of course, the price fluctuates wildly depending on the supply. In the fall of 2009, much of northern Sonora suffered through a horrible drought, leaving much of those involved in the business searching for another supply of chiltepines or considering other forms of work.

Though many have attempted to "domesticate" the chiltepin and grow it in a commercial setting, the nature of this fickle pepper makes it difficult to cultivate. Too much moisture leaves it susceptible to fungal infections. While resistant to drought, the chiltepin lacks natural resistance to diseases that invade row crops, for they evolved in extremely low densities.

While not overt, the influence of the chiltepin can be seen throughout the Sonoran Desert region. Tables are set with small bowls of dried chiltepin to crumble on top of the plate of the day. The baseball team of Baviacora, in the Rio Sonora Valley, is called the Chiltepineros. During years of plenty, impromptu stands and speed-bump merchants hawk their wares. Chiltepines can be found on amulets to ward away spirits and in herbal cures. Much like trying to find the chiltepin plants in the desert, it takes an adjustment of vision to see the chiltepin in Sonoran daily life. But once you get that chile vision homed in, you'll see it everywhere you go.

Kraig

times. Chiltepin foraging, at least for now and in some particular places, appears to have a bit more capacity to recover from catastrophic events than industrial agriculture—even the kind of small-scale mechanized, irrigated agriculture of citrus being attempted by Sergio, Oscar, and Chano. Nevertheless, most wild chiltepin harvesters and merchandisers were in hot water back in 2009.

The last stop of the Spice Ship in Sonora brought us to the southern edges of that state, to the great historic colonial town of Alamos. There, amid streets lined with palms and colorful guamúchil trees, Guarijio Indians seasonally arrive from their haunts way up in the Sierra Madre Occidental to offer their harvests of chiltepines to local vendors. But that traditional pilgrimage hardly happened during the latter months of 2009. Like the north, far southern Sonora was hit with a drought so fierce that the wild chile crop *completely* failed in many localities.

"Not a single bag of chiltepines arrived from Guarijio Indian territory this year," spice market vendor Hugo Sesta explained to us. He was surrounded by bags of wild oregano, medicinal herbs, and such but had only a few bottles of dried chiltepines from the 2008 harvest to sell.

"There were so few produced in the entire region this last year, a very small harvest, and very late even where they did produce something outside the Guarijio zone. Well, they're from the wild, and get no pampering, so they produce very little some years. Two years ago, when there was a bumper crop, I could buy them from the harvesters for 350 pesos per kilo. This year, I couldn't get the few that were offered to me for less than 800 pesos per kilo. So I didn't buy any of them; they cost too much for my customers to even want to purchase them . . ."

In a seed and spice shop around the corner from Hugo's farmer's market booth, spice trader Fernando Niño Estudillo was even more distressed about the scarcity of chiltepines, for he typically runs tons of them up to the border, to be sold on the US side of the line.

"I've been ten years in the business; most years I drive truckloads of chiltepines to Tijuana myself. Only this last year has the wild chile crop ever failed me . . . I didn't even make a single trip up to the border . . ."

As Gary heard Fernando lament this sudden shift in his business income, he remembered the words he had heard from an eminent desert scientist just a few months before. Daniel Hillel, who was among the first to speculate about the effects of climate change on desert agriculture, had this to say to Gary:

"With climate change, there will inevitably be gainers and losers, because there will be places where growing conditions become more favorable for particular crops, and places where growing conditions will deteriorate for other food plants. Essentially the effects in any particular place are not yet very predictable!"

As we sailed our Spice Ship back across the border, we ruminated over the take-home message of our first trip together as gastronauts: As the global climate changes, it is affecting different places just a few miles apart in very different ways. One patch of chiles might survive a storm, while another not too far away is washed clean off the face of the earth. Unless we can find a way to live with that basic fact, it will be hard for any of us—chiles included—to adapt, let alone survive.

## Poblanos Rellenos with Grilled Shrimp

This dish is from the province of Puebla, just south of Mexico City, where the namesake poblano chile reigns supreme. When ripened, roasted, and dried, the poblano is referred to as an ancho chile, and it is commonly strung on decorative *ristras* throughout Mexico.

In its fresh, deep green form, it's ideal for roasting and stuffing. Mild compared with many of the chiles we discuss here, the poblano does pack a little heat. It is moderated further in this dish through roasting and by removing the stem, pith, and seeds.

To roast this (or any) chile, it's helpful to have a grill or a gas range, though the broiler in your oven can suffice. Place the whole chiles over a high, direct flame. No pot or pan, just directly on the gas burner or the grill. In only a couple of minutes, they will begin to burn and blister (that's good, it's what you want). As each side gets charred, turn the pepper to the next side and so on, until it is blistered and charred entirely. Drop the pepper in a paper bag and roll the bag sealed like you would a sack lunch. Repeat with all the chiles you are roasting, and let them rest in the bag for fifteen minutes or so. Remove them to a cutting board and, using a paring knife, gently scrape away the now-loosened skin, revealing the thick flesh.

Then, with the point of the paring knife, make an incision into the shoulder of the pepper adjacent to the stem. Cut around the stem, then gently remove it and the attached seedpod. Carefully cut away the remaining pith and straggling seeds and your pepper is ready to stuff. A pastry bag is handy for that, but a spoon can work if you are patient.

Most rellenos you see in restaurants are battered and fried, but for reasons of both health and simplicity, this one is baked. Serve it with a walnut cream sauce and pomegranate seeds and you have chiles en nogada, the traditional dish of Mexican Independence Day with its flag colors of green, white, and red.

> **12 large shrimp, grilled (or quickly sautéed) and cooled**
> **1 tablespoon minced garlic**
> **¼ cup chopped fresh cilantro**
> **1 egg**
> **1 cup *queso fresco* (or substitute ricotta)**
> **1 lime, juiced**
> **½ cup fine dried bread crumbs**
> **Salt and pepper to taste**
> **4 poblano chiles, roasted and peeled, stem and seeds removed**

Chop the grilled shrimp fine, and combine with the garlic, cilantro, egg, *queso fresco* or ricotta, lime juice, and bread crumbs. Mix well. Taste and adjust the seasoning with salt and pepper.

Using a piping bag, fill the roasted chiles with the cheese mixture. Pinch closed and secure each opening with a toothpick. Lay out on a sheet pan and roast at 400°F for 8 to 10 minutes, or until heated through. Serve immediately. *Serves 4.*

## Carne Machaca con Verduras de Sonora

One of the reasons chiles gained popularity around the globe so quickly after being brought to the Old World from the New is their usefulness as a preservative for meat. Of course, drying meat had already long been a practice in these same cultures; combining the two strategies must have seemed what we now refer to as a no-brainer.

This recipe is, in a sense, a more rustic (and genuine) version of the fajitas popularized in modern chain restaurants across the United States. It utilizes *machaca*, a form of dried beef brisket popular in the Sonoran Desert of north-central Mexico and southern Arizona. It is, in essence, what Americans would call jerky. My grandpa used to call it "cowboy meat" due to its ubiquitous presence in saddlebags in the Old West. It retains its popularity for similar uses to this day. For purposes such as the recipe below, it is widely available pre-shredded.

Gary's fondness for this dish of his adopted homeland, which he affectionately refers to as "The Stinkin' Hot Desert," mandates its inclusion here, but it would have been necessary anyway for its foundational use of the cherished chiltepin in two forms—dry and red as well as fresh and green. Adjust the heat level to your tastes by adding or omitting as many as you wish.

A note about nopales—the leaves or pads of the genus *Opuntia* from the Cactaceae family, or what is commonly known as the prickly pear cactus. It is widely available in bodegas and should be obtained as fresh as possible. Spring and summer are the common harvest times, so look for them then. Wash them thoroughly and boil or grill them for any number of uses. The boiled option often produces a certain mucilaginous texture many people find objectionable, so my preference is grilled.

And about the amaranth: Its leaves are a common vege-table throughout many parts of Africa, Asia, and Central and South America. It is often referred to as *quelite* or pigweed, and is quite tasty and nutritious. If it is unavailable, you might substi-tute less authentic (but still delicious) spinach leaves.

1½ cups shredded *carne machaca*
2 cups water
4 red chiltepines, dried and crushed
2 tablespoons extra-virgin olive oil
8–12 green chiltepines, chopped
3 tablespoons dried Mexican oregano
1 cup grilled and diced *nopales*
2–3 cups chopped *quelite* (wild amaranth) leaves
1 medium white onion, peeled and diced
1 garlic clove, peeled and sliced paper-thin
1 sprig cilantro
6–8 tomatillos, husks removed, coarsely chopped

Soak the shredded meat in the water with the red chiltepines for at least 1 hour up to overnight. Drain off the excess water. Alternatively, simply simmer for about 10 minutes.

Heat the oil in a sauté pan over medium heat. Add the green chiltepines and sauté, being careful about the fumes, which can burn or choke you if directly inhaled. When the chiltepines are tender (3–5 minutes), add the oregano, grilled *nopales, quelite* leaves, onion, garlic, and cilantro, and sauté stirring, until the onion is browned.

Add the tomatillos and soaked meat and continue to cook, stirring, for another 5 minutes or until the tomatillos have soft-ened. Taste for salt, although usually the dried meat provides plenty.

Serve with flour tortillas and a side of pinto or tepary beans. *Serves 2–4.*

# CHAPTER TWO

# The Datil Pepper: First Chile of the First Coast

**THE THREE GASTRONAUTS** arrived in Jacksonville, Florida, unsure of what we would find on this particular leg of our spice odyssey. We were after the datil pepper this time. Although each of us had some previous experience with this heirloom chile, we had never encountered it in its home environs, so we were eager to explore its cultural nursery grounds. Through our various affiliations and work with Slow Food USA, we had been part of the effort to get the datil pepper "boarded" on the Ark of Taste as a food of significant culinary value that was in danger of being lost from its culture. The Ark of Taste is the most iconic of all the Slow Food biodiversity initiatives. In a few words, it is a platform to try and promote varieties, breeds, and other foods that have important historic and cultural connections before they are lost.

But how could a food become endangered? And what does it mean when we say that a food has been lost? According to the Food and Agriculture Organization of the United Nations (the FAO), in the last century three-quarters of our foodstuffs have disappeared from farms and gardens worldwide, such that consumers no longer have access to them in the marketplace. In North America, at least two-thirds of the crops grown on this continent in prehistoric times can no longer be found in gardens and fields anywhere in the world; either they have been replaced by modern varieties, or the fields themselves have been developed into subdivisions, schools, industrial plants, or parks. Across the entire spectrum of food crops, from apples to zucchini, the story is the same. Diversity has been sacrificed to meet the exigent demands of the globalized food distribution system—uniformity, expediency, "efficiency," and shipability. Why pay more money for one of the fifteen thousand apple varieties that once graced American orchards when you can get a real deal on Red Delicious or Fujis that were shipped all the way from China—perhaps laced with arsenic to control pests?

And yet the industrialization and supermarketization of our food system, though rightly receiving the brunt of the blame, are not the sole causes of diminishing diversity in our food system. Many heirloom crop varieties have always been localized specialties, with limited ranges and very specific adaptations to a particular place. This inherently makes them rare, regardless of whether there are threats from development, diseases, or pests.

The datil pepper was indeed rare in this sense, and we were there in Florida to understand something about the severity of the threats to its continued survival. It appeared that there were just a few commercial datil growers, and most of them were found in the coastal lowlands surrounding St. Augustine—a very limited geographic area, and one that may be increasingly vulnerable to rising ocean levels and more ferocious tropical storms. Yet none of us was sure that these preconceived notions were valid. We had heard and read a lot about the datil, but only now were we getting the chance to "ground-truth" these notions here in the stretch of northern Florida popularly referred to as the First Coast.

It's called the *First* Coast for a good reason: This stretch of beaches and waterways on the Floridian peninsula is thought to have been visited in 1513 by Ponce de León, who, according to apocryphal legend, was searching for the mythical Fountain of Youth. While the exact sites of his landing and the elusive fountain remain historical enigmas, Ponce de

León is still hailed as the first European explorer to this coast, predating any other English, Spanish, or French explorers who surveyed the southernmost realm of the Atlantic seaboard.

Nevertheless, Ponce de León left no legacy of permanent settlements. That honor goes to Pedro Menéndez de Avilés, who, in 1565, founded the port town of St. Augustine after engaging in a fierce territorial battle with the French navy. The port has since weathered many a storm, making it the oldest continuously inhabited European settlement in the United States.

Now, St. Augustine may be the heart and soul of the First Coast, but to get to it we had to get past Jacksonville, one of the largest metropolitan flash-in-the-pan sprawl zones in all of Florida. The rates of land development and habitat loss occurring in and around Jacksonville in just the last half century are of staggering proportions.

Jacksonville has become the one of the most overdeveloped, high-density recreational havens in the United States, but an altogether different place with a distinctively different ambience can be found by veering just a couple of miles off the interstate to the south of that metropolis. There you can still find Florida Crackers, the descendants of the original American settlers to Florida. Today the term *Cracker* is used less pejoratively than it once was to distinguish a certain strain of multigenerational southerners from the newcomers. In some communities, the word is used with pride to identify the backwater curmudgeons of the region who have found a way to maintain some modicum of continuity with Florida's wild past.

Not only do Crackers defend their home ground from obvious assaults, but their healthy respect for the land comes from living with it. They still hunt, fish, garden, propagate, and forage native plants with a certain gusto. They know their local history cold because they and their ancestors have lived it. They keep alive stories passed down directly from the old-timers, whether they be Native American, Minorcan, black, or Cracker. While not many Crackers would necessarily self-identify as conservationists, a certain number of them are nevertheless engaged with some of the oddest coalitions found anywhere in America, all fighting to keep the natural and cultural uniqueness of their home place intact.

Datil peppers are part of that cultural uniqueness. And yet, because of our unfamiliarity with the First Coast, we weren't sure whether the datil pepper was simply rare relative to Florida's many other crops, or whether family farms themselves were becoming an endangered species in the state, or whether both cases were true. As we sailed the Spice Ship down the interstate a few miles inland from the coast, we saw a few farms, but shopping malls, fast-food outlets, housing developments, raceways, and golf courses easily outnumbered them. A quick check of USDA data showed that some Florida counties had slipped from 42 percent of their arable land area in food production at the end of World War II to less than 4 percent today. It sobered us to realize that few of Florida's heirloom vegetables will have any home to speak of in the future as long as the state's loss of farmland continues at its current average pace—thirty-seven hundred acres per year.

Certainly, coastal Florida is not the only place in America where fields and orchards are rapidly being converted to urban, suburban, and rural recreational uses. At least a dozen other states have suffered more severe losses of farmland in recent years—for instance, California has seen one of every six acres of its farmlands developed since the days of the Gold Rush in the mid-nineteenth century. Florida, with the highest number of golf courses of any state in the United States, has its own lavish and ostentatious way of wasting food-producing lands. (Anyone willing to try a salad of fescue and zoysia turf greens?)

As we were about to see firsthand, coastal Florida is chimerical, appearing as two different places at the very same time. As one long-term resident later explained to us, the two Floridas coexist, but residents tend to live in either one or the other. There are those who prefer the Floridian manifestations of Anywhere, USA, and those who propagate and cultivate the culture and the history of the First Coast. Floridians still have a choice. You can eat factory food, detached from its roots and trucked in to chain restaurants, or you can sample Florida's own datil peppers, its pompano, pilau (pronounced *PER-low*), shrimp, Seminole pumpkins, clams, yams, coonti, snook, smoked mullet, Cracker Cattle beef, and conch fritters. You can allow Florida to float away as world ocean levels rise a projected three to five feet by the year 2100, moving the shoreline an average of three thousand feet farther inland. Or you can take a stand on a little patch of land and attempt to protect the hell out of it.

Perhaps no one exemplifies this latter stance better than the host for our sojourn into Florida's First Coast, Bill Hamilton. Bill is the co-owner and operator of Southern Horticulture, a garden shop and landscaping business that strongly favors native plants. He is also a passionate activist, food producer, local historian, conservation planner, and informal educator.

Bill is one of those rare kinds of people that each community in the world desperately needs, for he seems to get things done for the common good, whether or not there is any money or bureaucratic support to do so, and never seeks the credit afterward. Bill may be close to sixty, but he is still lean, athletic, radical in his thinking, and at the same time unapologetically fun loving.

On top of that, he makes a pretty mean datil pepper hot sauce. As does his brother, Pat. As does his wife, Bryanne. As does his sister-in-law, Jean Dowdy. And no two of the family recipes are quite the same. Datil sauce is usually a tomato-based concoction, with differing heats and interpretations; some versions tend to be sweet and acidic, but all of them have that special datil touch. While Bill and Pat used most of the same basic ingredients, their sauces were as different as they come.

Within hours of getting into the St. Augustine area, we were happily ensconced in the Hamilton kitchen in Crescent Beach, trying out hot sauces, fresh vegetables, wines, and other local fare. After each family member got around to telling how they made their own peculiar version of datil pepper hot sauce, the conversation drifted on to other topics. We asked Bill if he personally had observed any signs that shifting weather patterns may be starting to affect life on the First Coast.

"Did you say *starting* to affect us around here?" He paused for a moment to offer us a grin that kindly acknowledged that we clearly were not from these parts. Bill then carefully chose his next few words.

"Changes in the climate are *already* pretty hard on us. Hurricanes? Winds from tropical storms? Rising temperatures? We've already got it all! Especially the intensity of rain events. Summer heat is more intense, too. And we don't get those intense freezes in the winter that we used to get somewhere in Florida nearly every year. The whole [First Coast] ecosystem that historically generated the trade winds that brought the Spanish conquistadores back and forth used to be *right here,* and now it's gone. Look at where the citrus was grown. St. Augustine was once the center of citrus. We had a lot of citrus all around the town. Then we had such a catastrophic freeze event that the center of citrus production moved at least a hundred miles south. Now it's warming up around here, and so some are replanting citrus."

Bill continued in a broader vein: "For many plants, this was either the southern or northern limits for their species. Now those limits have shifted. And new pests have come in. In fact, the impacts from these new pests are getting to be *way* over the top . . ."

Bill's wife, Bryanne, could see that his blood pressure was starting to rise, so she quickly and nimbly changed the subject, calling us into the kitchen to help put her wonderfully prepared mélange of local foods on the dining room table. Bill calmed down and winked at us. Then he whispered to Gary, "Don't you all worry. We'll get into this *big time* when we visit Mark Barnes's farm later in the week. For now, let's just have some fun." We did that with no trouble, thanks to Bryanne's fabulous food and the entire family's capacity for storytelling.

The next day, we went to historic downtown St. Augustine to look on St. George Street between Cuna and Hipolita Streets for further clues as to the origin of datil peppers on the First Coast. We were looking for the house of the man who reputedly introduced datil peppers to the First Coast. The stories of the origin and introduction of the datil pepper are numerous and have reached mythic proportions among some of the locals. The most recent reinterpretation has benefited from the work of a diligent historian, David Nolan. Mr. Nolan's sleuthing uncovered a June 13, 1937, article in the *St. Augustine Record* that documented the then-known origins of the arrival of the datil pepper to St. Augustine. The article states that in the mid-1880s, a "Spaniard" named Estevan (or Stephen) B. Valls, who produced jellies, jams, and marmalades through his small local business, had sent for seeds of the datil pepper, which was growing in Santiago, Cuba, at that time.

The datil of Santiago was a kin to the habanero of the Yucatán; both belong to the pepper species first described in 1776 as *Capsicum chinense*. The seeds must have arrived from Santiago in the mid-1880s, and at first Valls planted them only in his yard on St. George Street. His place in the historic district—known locally for decades as the Lorillard Place—is still owned by one of his descendants, and sits amid all the gorgeous restored homes and tourist shops that feature the unique heritage of the First Coast.

Once Valls had gotten the seeds to germinate, the pepper plants grew exceedingly well on St. George Street and on farmlands edging St. Augustine. Soon Valls's friends asked for some of his seeds to sow in Daytona Beach and New Smyrna. As datil peppers became more integrated into the local cuisine of the area, they were quickly adopted into the dishes of one of the distinct cultural groups of the area—the descendents of Minorcan settlers. The island of Minorca has played a rather exceptional role in the history of St. Augustine, and continues to do so today. After the Minorcan community claimed the datil as their own, the link to Cuba through Valls was largely forgotten. The Minorcan community developed so much affection for the datil pepper that they incorporated it as one of their cultural icons and signifiers, and their oral history claimed it as one of the original plants brought by Minorcan settlers with them in 1768. While that latter assertion has not stood the test of time, it is clear that the Minorcans now covet their datil-based culture and cuisine.

In any case, the use of datil peppers is one of several key features that now define Minorcan-American cuisine in the First Coast. By the time Marjorie Kinnan Rawlings began to compile the uses of datil peppers in sauces and chowders for her mouthwatering book *Cross Creek Cookery*, published in 1942, she found that her Minorcan neighbors had elaborated many distinctive recipes that incorporate datils, including a tomato-based seafood chowder that featured gopher tortoise as the meat.

By Rawlings's era, the seeds of this heirloom pepper were being passed hand to hand, family to family, and had become cherished among both Minorcan and Cracker families. These cultural communities are among those on the First Coast that still celebrate their connections to the heirloom peppers in local festivals such as the St. Ambrose Parish Fair. The fair has been held for more than 120 years along the Moccasin Branch in the small town of Elkton, not far from St. Augustine. There a locally renowned cook named Mary Ellen Masters has become the reigning "Master of Minorcan Clam Chowder." For the festival alone, she cooks up over 150 gallons of chowder. She serves her cherished chowder alongside a Minorcan pork pilau, steamed cabbage, hobo ribs, and, of course, datil pepper sauce.

Following our visit to pay homage to Señor Valls on St. George Street, we searched out just about every venue that sells datil pepper products in the St. Augustine area, hoping to get a sense of how deep datil fever runs in the region. For a pepper that has hardly been grown or even eaten much in other parts of the country, it was talked about on the First Coast as though the entire world *should* know about it but doesn't quite get its significance. Marcia McQuaig mentioned this to us when we called her up to schedule an appointment with her at the Minorcan Datil Pepper Products headquarters for later in the day.

"I'm glad you boys from out of state have heard about us and our datil peppers. It's odd around here; when you get across that Florida state line into Georgia going toward Atlanta, and you try to talk to them about all of this, they'll say, *Now, what's a datil?* However, once people have tried the hot sauce, they're hooked. They'll buy caseloads. Ain't it funny? You don't have to get too far beyond St. John's County, Florida, and simply no one has even seen what a datil pepper looks like unless they grew up here then moved to somewhere else. We need to tell them that we're not talking about *just another* hot sauce, we're talking about [a food tradition with] four hundred years of history . . ."

The four-hundred-year legacy Marcia refers to is that of the Minorcan community around St. Augustine, Elkton, and Hastings, whose ancestors brought with them from the island of Minorca a distinctive culinary sensibility forged from Spanish, Greek, and Phoenician influences. The Minorcans arrived in the late 1700s, agreeing to come to Florida and work on an indigo plantation in New Symrna, just to the south of St. Augustine, in exchange for land and opportunity. After a few years, the conditions on the plantation had deteriorated, and the Minorcans fled to the north, asking for sanctuary in the town of St. Augustine, where they became part of the fabric of the town. Long after datil peppers had become key ingredients in the home-style Minorcan chowders and pilaus, a few Minorcan families started to produce their datil sauces for sale at local festivals and roadside stands.

The datil pepper stayed below the radar of most Americans—except those lucky Florida Crackers and Minorcans—until a local entrepreneur named Chris Way began to publicize its uniqueness. Drawing upon his experience with tourist-oriented restaurants and mail-order businesses, Way promoted the first datil pepper hot sauce to sell beyond the First Coast, the iconic Datil-Do-It hot sauce. Datil-Do-It was a great success and inspired other locals to market and sell their own datil-inspired products.

As we made our rounds that first crisp but sunny morning on the coast, we ran into a younger local entrepreneur named Mike Martin at his storefront outlet for Datil Daddy Beef Jerky. Mike loves to promote pepper products other than his own, as he had shelves full of different varieties of datil pepper sauces, but he gave Chris credit for getting the ball rolling some two decades before he himself started up his own business.

"Chris Way was *the man* for datil peppers. He's the one that put datil peppers on the map. But given all its notoriety today, it's still not truly a commercial [commodity] pepper, by no means. Not like a jalapeño or a tabasco. It is *rare*. Datil peppers are close to being on the extinct [*sic*] list because there're just not that many growers. I mean, some people keep only two or three plants in big ol' pots that they keep for making their own sauce at home, but if I didn't have access to some eight hundred other plants grown for me by my friend Jack, I wouldn't be able to maintain any level of commercial production. *That's right* . . . We need *more* growers."

When we later mentioned what Mike Martin had said to us about the paucity of growers, Marcia McQuaig agreed. Over the years she's been in the business, the old-timers growing more than just a few pots of datil plants seem to have declined: "Today there are still not enough peppers to go around. The few experienced growers left are really struggling. It's just too labor-intensive—it takes two whole hours to pick a bushel of datil peppers. And on top of that, weather conditions have wreaked havoc on us. In 2004, as all the storms rolled in, the wind whipped all the containers around and beat the bushes all to hell. That's when some people who had been growing them for years just got up and checked *out*."

There is still farmland between St. Augustine, Crescent Beach, and Hastings, but the roadside fruit stands that historically sold citrus and local vegetables such as fresh datils in season no longer carry them on a regular basis. The average farmers and gardeners in these parts come in shades of gray, for most of them are pushing sixty or seventy years of age. Much of the best farmland has been sold off over the last few decades, turned into new housing developments and their associated golf courses. Other farms converted to growing sod for the new developments, only to have the market collapse a couple of years later. Fewer farmers, fewer farms, fewer peppers—it is a simple equation.

We met up with Bill after his morning chores were done so that he could drive us out past Hastings to the midscale farm of Mark Barnes. Bill was hoping that seeing Mark's operation would help us gain a sense of the overall context of vegetable farming on the First Coast. Unlike other farmers we later visited, Mark doesn't specialize in datil peppers. Instead, he grows a wide variety of vegetables and vine fruits for larger produce distributors, often working with their brokers on direct contracts.

Within minutes of sitting down with Mark, we realized that it was virtually impossible to get away from the issues of changing weather, as well as changing distributions of weeds, pests, and diseases along the First Coast. It was as Bill had hinted at the dinner table: These issues are not trivial for First Coast farmers, for they affect them *big time.*

Mark Barnes does not grow vegetables in pots like a hobbyist. He farms hundreds of acres intensively, sometimes harvesting several crops from the same acre over the course of a year. The way he described farming sounded like he was describing a boxing match—absorbing some straight rights to the head, making him woozy and thinking about throwing in the towel, but standing tall and getting in his own licks at other times as well. He's a big man with an expressive face that is as deeply furrowed as his fields, and you might say that farming has given Mark a *worried mind.* But as Bill had previously suggested to us, Mark is a keen observer of nature's changes, especially those that have affected most farmers along the First Coast. He was an ideal starting point for us in our initial attempts to fathom all the factors that are having an impact on datil peppers and the families that have farmed them.

We met in Mark's mobile office building, which is perched on blocks above one of his larger fields, in a clearing in the forest. Mark tapped a pencil on the desk in front of him as he spoke, tapping harder whenever he wanted to drive home a particular point. When we asked him about the weather—a favorite subject of most farmers—the topic quickly morphed from the meteorological alone to the ecological and economic.

"What's changed here more than anything over my lifetime is the *severity* of cold—not just here, but over much of the South. See, farmers in Georgia are now my competition, and they didn't used to be. Our winters used to be milder than theirs. But the way the weather has been the last ten to fifteen years, they're now able to grow the same things that I can grow and have it to market just as early as I can. They just couldn't do that before. Georgia did get hit last year, I know, but we ourselves haven't had any really severe cold for about fifteen years."

He stopped talking for a minute and tried to pull up some dates from his mental hard drive. The phone was ringing off the hook, but he ignored it. He tapped his pencil twice, then started in again.

"It must have been in the early 1980s that we had the last cold snap that killed most of the orange trees all the way down to Orlando. And 1964 was last time we had a real direct hit from a hurricane, and that was from Dora.

"But what we suffered last year was pretty damn tough even though it wasn't a direct hit. A tropical storm just *sat* here. The damn thing put down *tweeent-tee-four* inches of rain right on top of us. My soils usually drain off quickly, but this time we were flooded. My fruit was *floating*. My entire cantaloupe crop was actually floating away, my investment down the tubes. When we rescued them, we initially thought there was actually nothing wrong with the fruit. They looked all right; you could go ahead and eat 'em if you wanted to, right then and there. But when you shook one of them melons, it sounded like a coconut. Some of them did get kinda hollow like a coconut, but that's after they had turned soft and mealy inside, 'cause the water content went way up with the floods that followed the storm.

"But here's the thing. When a broker, like a buyer for Walmart, comes here and he picks up *just one* of my melons and it sounds hollow like that—if it sounds like a coconut—*I'm a goner,* I lose my shirt. My entire crop is worth nothing at all in the marketplace anymore."

Before he could continue, Mark's staff insisted that he take an important phone call, and then another. We sat with Bill and tried to put into context what Mark had just said. Bill added as much perspective as he could, without having the exact numbers from Mark's good and bad years: "Here's this guy, Mark, with as much savvy as anyone around here has in terms of how to adapt to an ever-changing market. And then some storm comes along and nearly knocks him out of the ring. I thought he was gonna hafta throw in the towel. But Mark came back, though the immediate effects of that one storm aren't all that he's had to face over the long haul."

Mark was back from the phone call and picked up his cue from Bill. "Sure, it just goes on and on. I now got weeds we never used to have. I don't know all their names, you know, some of 'em are new to this area. But they're pretty tough, like Florida *pusley* . . . now that one has gotten *bad*. We've seen it here in the field this year for the first time ever.

"And weeds aren't the only thing. I'll tell you another thing what we all gotta be concerned about . . . that's the *bees.* I'm telling you they've got a prob-*lem*. The beekeeper I work with, he had three hundred hives that started to die on him just when they got them out here this last year. We usually put out every one of his three hundred hives, about one and a half hives for every acre of crops. But as soon as he dropped them off here last year, those bees started going *down* . . ."

Aside from direct hits by hurricanes, Mark and his neighbors have recently suffered windstorms, floods, washed-in weed seeds, higher summer temperatures, periodic catastrophic freezes, diseases, pests, and declining bee populations. We were beginning to see that farmers are witnessing, and in some cases suffering from, changes in the land that defy some tidy textbook definition of *global climate change*. What is difficult to discern is which of these changes may be primarily *driven* by accelerated climate change, and which are *triggered* by unusual weather events that may or may not have anything to do with long-term trends.

While scientists debate about the direct links and the causes and effects, farmers like Mark Barnes simply try to adapt to this year's conditions. By the time the scientific experts have figured out these links and causes, though, it will be too late for the farmers, who will already be facing some new, as-yet-unknown challenges.

Like Mark Barnes, other farmers keenly observe certain kinds of correlations, quickly associating the appearance of a weed or pest with a particular landmark storm. They don't necessarily have time to figure out whether the tropical storm itself actually carried a new weed or disease into their fields, because they are forced to jump into the fight, trying to reduce the impacts of that uninvited newcomer on their bottom line.

But one take-home message from our conversation with Mark Barnes continued to reemerge wherever else we took the Spice Ship on our odyssey: The unanticipated appearances of noxious weeds, deadly viruses, or swarms of crop-consuming insects can potentially have devastating consequences for farmers. These are not abstractions; they are royal pains in the ass to deal with. If heirloom crops like datil peppers have never previously been exposed to particular diseases or pests, they may have no resistance at all to them. And if these heirlooms falter under such new pressures, we may incrementally lose more elements of the overall diversity of agriculture on the North American continent.

Achieving long-term food security may hinge on keeping that diversity in our fields. But it seems that this "hinge" is coming off the door, for it has suffered so many different assaults. We knew that vicious hurricanes, lingering droughts, and massive floods get most of the press about how climate change impacts our food supply, but we had begun to hear from farmers themselves of a far more nuanced and complex situation.

From Mark Barnes's position, you didn't have to be smashed by a Hurricane Rita or Katrina to be knocked out of the ring. A whole onslaught of other, more subtle effects could wear you down, like taking a number of body blows that end up dropping you to the mat.

Late in the afternoon, we made it over to see the McQuaigs at Minorcan Datil headquarters, where Marcia had a whole series of datil pepper products ready for our tasting. Her husband, Steve, of distinguished Minorcan descent, was there with her, and just as active in our discussion. Steve loves the flavor of datil peppers nearly as much as Marcia does, but he is quick to admit that a lot can go wrong quickly, based on his experience of growing his own datil peppers.

"The trouble with the storms around here is that they don't even have to be direct hits to mess up our pepper production. The 2004 hurricanes just brushed right by us, but they still generated seventy-mile-an-hour winds. As their gusts whipped up and the rains got stronger, it just tore the shreds out of our plants.

"I had fifty datil pepper plants I was growing out back here at the time. The soil is sandy here, with good drainage, and any standing water typically drains off pretty quick, so we don't have much trouble here with floods. But when the water just stood there in between the rows of pepper plants, I knew I was gonna lose all fifty. They were either gonna be stunted or they weren't comin' back *at all*. That's when I *quit* . . ."

We later heard a similar story from chef David Bearl about his own failed attempt at a datil pepper garden. Bearl runs the Southeast Institute of Culinary Arts at First Coast Technical College with consummate skill, but he sheepishly admitted that his skill set did not extend to keeping datil plants alive in his own backyard.

"Oh, I tried to grow my own datil pepper plants at home. I wouldn't say they're finicky, but it's just that when you get thirty inches of rain in three days like we did not too far back, I can tell you what will happen to most of us: Our doggone plants will all get sick. All of mine died."

Marcia McQuaig conjured up her own version of doom: "Just one afternoon thunderstorm or one fluky hailstorm can beat 'em to death. And we had not one, but *five tropical storms* in one year . . . It was picking and processing time and all the electricity went out and Steve was trying to get the lights and fans to work again with a generator. Like most Minorcans, he grew up pretty much learning how to fix anything he put his mind to, but even he was struggling to keep our facility going. And here I was trying to do all this work with the peppers before everything spoiled and it was so hot and humid. Finally, Steve got the power running just in time, or we wouldn't have produced anything that year . . .

"And that didn't just happen to *us*. Boy, have our custom growers struggled to come up with a decent crop year after year. Anyone who is willing to grow peppers for me, I tell them I'll take all we can get from them. There are not enough peppers to go around by a long shot, so I worry that some of the little pepper businesses around here may be forced to use peppers other than datils in their products. If they still choose to call them datil pepper sauces, there will be a heap of trouble. That won't be good for any of us."

There was just enough daylight left before dinnertime for Marcia to run us over to the homestead of Randy Haire, the best custom grower of datil peppers she had ever known. That was not merely Marcia's opinion. The world-renowned Pepper Lady, the late Dr. Jean Andrews, relied heavily on Randy's knowledge when she wrote the first lengthy historical and botanical article on datil peppers. Jean, who passed away to Pepper Heaven in January 2010, held Randy Haire in the highest regard.

Randy greeted us, as did his hound dog, and they took us out to a clearing in the woods where he had his "fun" fooling around with datil peppers. As he began to talk, our first impression was that he was rather amusing in how he described his casual way of growing datils. But that was all just self-effacing humor. When we saw how painstakingly elegant and productive Randy's pepper patch looked, we realized he was feigning that he was no more than a laid-back amateur. His plants were still growing and bearing fruit, immaculately maintained in big plastic pots fed by a drip irrigation system.

Randy had come up with a special soil mix that made him quite proud. He admitted that he did grow the peppers for the substantial sums of money they could bring in during a good harvest season, but he still insisted that he mainly grew them for the pleasure of it. Nevertheless, he had recently re-rigged his entire growing system so that it would be less vulnerable to the kind of horrendous winds that had nearly sent him running a few years before.

"The 2005 hurricanes beat hell out of my datil pepper plants," he told us. "It just ruined my greenhouse over there. You wouldn't think it just looking at how modest it is, but I had to put four thousand more dollars back into it to get it up and running. I was gonna quit for a while. I was down to keeping just fifty datil pepper plants, but now I want to get up to five hundred plants again. Why? Yeah, I suppose I need something to drive me nuts. *Trying to growing datil peppers around here will drive anyone nuts!*"

Randy grinned as he went on. So, it seemed, did his dog.

"First off, they don't like the heat. They get over ninety degrees and they don't even want to bloom. No, it's not because of some virus or wilt that comes with heat stress—they just plain don't *want* to bloom when it's hot.

"Next off, these things collect stink bugs *bad*. And they don't like wet feet. I gotta keep their roots well drained in these pots that I keep up off the ground, 'cause if they're just planted in the dirt, if there'd be a flood, I'll get fungus in all their roots.

"I've already had to get rid of one kind of a fungus disease that blew in with the storms. Hell, it's not only in the peppers, that wind-blown virus got into all the trees you see around here. And then, you remember hearin' on the news about all those thrips that came in from Africa, landin' here in Florida? Well, I believe that just about all of them thrips that came over from Africa ended up landing right here. I mean *right* here. Now, *that* was a trip—spraying for thrips so small you could hardly see the little suckers.

"Now then, if you think these recent hurricanes were bad, well, Dora in 1964 was the absolute worst. My old man was playin' poker all night and I was just a kid, playin' under the table. We heard a storm was a-comin', and then the walls started to tremble and shake like they were gonna *move*. Because it was already dark, we didn't even take a look outside, and my father just kept on playing poker. In the morning, we all crept up to the door with him and opened it to finally see what was going on out there. Just as we did, a fifty-gallon drum came a-sailin' by the door like it was a rocket."

Randy started chuckling, like something had plucked his funny bone. The rest of us couldn't help but laugh, too.

"Well, ol' Dora, she was just too much a wild woman for my old man. He closed the door tight and went back into the kitchen. We hid under the table just watchin' those walls shake like the entire deal was gonna git carried away. He kept playin' poker, not even lookin' up, let alone outside, until Dora departed and all the commotion stopped."

It was nearing dusk, and we had to get back to Crescent Beach for a gathering that Bill Hamilton had planned to introduce us to local farmers and Slow Food First Coast members. We bid Randy and Marcia good-bye and headed back to the beach.

The entrance to Genung's Fish Camp wasn't much more than a hundred yards from the beach house that Bill had loaned us for our stay of a few days. Next to the door of the shack that served as its headquarters were hand-painted letters announcing LIVE BAIT/TACKLE/ ICE/BOILED PEANUTS/SMOKED MULLET. But the shack was not where the action was. It was "out back," where Bill and his brother, Pat, had constructed a huge campfire for grilling fish, burgers, steaks, or anything else that offered itself up. In this case, the specialty of the night had just been pulled off the flames. It was a big pot of Minorcan pilau, which a mustachioed Mr. Barnes himself had brought over from his own restaurant—Johnny's Kitchen in Hastings. Dozens of folks were already drinking beer and sampling homemade datil pepper chowders and hot sauces by the time we arrived. Bill had invited just about anyone and everyone—Minorcan, Seminole, Cracker, or black—whom he believed had something to share with us about datil peppers, farming, or the future of food in Florida.

Fish camps of this sort were where true Floridian food traditions still flourished. Dishes of all shapes and sizes appeared on two picnic tables, but most of the contents were home-grown, homemade, or hand-caught. The locals prided themselves on their fishing, foraging, cooking, or scavenging skills. Datil peppers were just one of several regional specialties being featured for the evening, among the alligator tail, smoked mullet, and fried mullet roe.

After everyone had had a chance to eat, drink, shake hands, and say howdy, Bill Hamilton introduced a remarkable Native American friend of his, a spiritual leader of Seminole ancestry, who blessed us and challenged us to take better care of the earth and its bounty. He then asked Richard "Cheech" Villadoniga, the leader of Slow Food First Coast, to say a few words about the fine work he had been doing to document the history of datils and other heritage foods. Cheech is an exceedingly bright young history teacher who spends much of his spare time traveling back roads through the South and meeting the old-time growers and processors of heirloom vegetables, gumbo filés, and other gustatory delights.

Bill and Cheech then introduced us to their community, and as the sun went down over the inland waterway we sat on stools and began a discussion with the seventy locals on the scene. They asked us to explain why we had come to St. Augustine, and why datil peppers—as well as other chiles—were of such interest to us.

"Well, we're using chiles as a lens for looking at how folks like you may be affected by climate change," Kraig explained. "People have this image of melting icebergs and drowning polar bears, but climate change is already affecting our food traditions and where certain crops can be grown. In the future, all that we know about modern farming might have to be reconsidered."

Kraig then told of his work on the Slow Food Biodiversity Committee, which had "boarded" the datil pepper onto the Ark of Taste to draw attention to its conservation needs and culinary qualities.

Kurt continued. "Chiles are the world's number one condiment," he reminded us. "From a chef's perspective, climate change might have a tremendous effect on how and what we eat in the future."

He explained why the decline and potential loss of heritage foods such as datil peppers is of concern to chefs across the country, who are always looking for the best and most flavorful ingredients to share with their communities.

Gary chimed in. "You have something special here you need to keep alive. But we're wondering how vulnerable a chile pepper like the datil might be to changing weather. It has such a narrow range, but such strong traditions associated with it. From what we heard from your neighbors today, erratic weather, pests, and diseases have been wreaking havoc with it in recent years."

He went on to tell about the larger collaborative effort involving Slow Food USA and other organizations, the Renewing America's Food Traditions alliance.

Our commentaries prompted several of the locals to testify about what they had been witnessing in their own fields and gardens, and what changes—both ecological and economic—worried them the most. After nearly an hour of animated discussion, we ended the more formal program and broke into smaller conversations around the campfire.

As the last of the party started to make its way back home (or on to the next gathering), we helped clean up and started to think about the great food that had been shared. Of course, that got us thinking and planning our very next meal . . .

"Rest up," Bill told us on our way out. "After you see what chef David Bearl and Eddie Lambert at First Coast Technical College are doing to make datil peppers more accessible to folks here on the First Coast, I'm goin' to take you to Johnny's Kitchen for lunch."

The next morning, we saw Eddie's massive grow-out of "starter plants" to help backyard producers ramp up datil pepper production in the area, and we heard about how the technical school's turfgrass program was slowly segueing into a horticultural/nursery program on the back of the datil pepper's success. We also learned that Chef David had recently served Minorcan pilau with datil peppers to presidential guests at the White House. But because we had already been given a tantalizing taste of what Johnny's cooking could be like, we were a bit distracted, perhaps overly eager to moor the Spice Ship in front of Mr. Barnes's restaurant in Hastings around noon.

It had become abundantly clear to us that Johnny Barnes was the real engine behind the revival of certain local food traditions along the First Coast. Born and raised by cotton sharecroppers, Johnny needed a few years to understand that home-style Cracker cooking was to be his true calling. After a stint with the navy, he ended up in northern California for a while, preparing haute cuisine in high-end restaurants and later serving as a personal chef for California celebrities. But after he finally returned to his roots in Hastings, he opened up a restaurant that combined First Coast food traditions with a bit of California's penchant for fresh and seasonal greens, vegetables, and fish.

If you have ever passed through Hastings, Florida, you might argue that it seems an unlikely epicenter for the First Coast's heritage food revival. At first glance, Hastings looks like just one more depopulated farm town in north Florida, replete with the crumbling remains of an agricultural supply store, a corner mini mart, a liquor store, and a Subway sandwich shop all nestled around the one stoplight at the

center of town. The once-numerous family farms have been consoli-
dated into just a few larger farms, which predominantly serve to deliver
produce to places in the United States other than the First Coast itself.

But Johnny Barnes is attempting to counter Hastings's historic brain
drain and outflow of agricultural assets. He is trying to make sure that
some of the tastiest food that is grown in and around Hastings stays *in
place,* for the enjoyment, nourishment, and betterment of his community. And the place where you can get the true taste of Hastings *is*
Johnny's Kitchen.

It is fairly unassuming from the outside, but wait until you open the
doors! The simple four-tops are filled with older gentlemen in their
high peaked mesh ballcaps lingering over coffee, and younger folks
trying to squeeze in a meal before going back to work. It is so packed
with locals that outsiders like us had a hard time finding a place to even
park our Spice Ship, and so we feared there would be no empty table.

But from behind the counter beckoned the iconic Johnny, a man
who is as physically large as his reputation. He was gesturing for us to get
over to an empty table he had saved for us before one of the locals with
well-established seniority got miffed that he couldn't sit there. Johnny's
sweeping handlebar mustache and his rather high-pitched voice—well,
higher than you'd expect from a six-foot-five man who carries nearly
three hundred pounds around on his Cracker bones—make him immediately endearing. But he wasn't there for self-aggrandizement; he simply
wanted to let the food speak for itself.

"We got fried pork chops, chicken and rice, or fried catfish with
your choice of two sides." Johnny nodded over toward the whiteboard,
which listed the daily array of available sides—mostly Southern classics
like field acre peas, butter beans, okra and tomatoes, and macaroni and
cheese.

"This fine young lady here will take care of you fellas." Johnny
announced his departure by nodding toward the waitress and headed
back to the kitchen for a while, checking in on some of the other
customers along the way. We placed our order and then began to look
around. Kraig immediately noticed that each table had a special basket

# Datil

## (*Capsicum chinense*)

The datil pepper is the *Capsicum chinense* country cousin to the more urbane and celebrated habanero pepper. While the habanero pepper has become synonymous with Yucatecan cuisine and heat, the datil pepper has become entwined with the history and culture of Florida's northern coast (known as the First Coast), and more specifically with descendants of Minorcan colonists.

One of the many myths of the datil pepper is that the original seeds were brought by the Minorcans themselves in the late 1700s. The Minorcans, along with a mélange of Greeks and Italians, had agreed to become colonists for a nascent indigo plantation on the coast of Florida. After arriving and working on the plantation for a couple of years, the new colonists had had enough. They escaped the repressive conditions of the plantation and fled to St. Augustine, where they were welcomed. The group settled there, where today, generations of Minorcan-descended Floridians have identified themselves through their ancestry—many tracing back their lineage to the original ship's registry—and through their cuisine and the use of the datil pepper. While the habanero has been cultivated only recently in the United States—and mostly in gardens by hobbyists—the datil pepper dates back to the 1880s, when it was brought from an unknown Cuban port. Since that time, the datil pepper, like other First Coast émigrés, has sunk its roots deep into the First Coast soil, and its history has become entwined with those long associated with St. Augustine and the colonization of this area.

A fully mature datil pepper plant is quite a sight: It can grow as tall as six feet, with the maturing yellow and orange peppers like pendant tongues of flame—St. Augustine's very own burning bush. Much like other varieties of *C. chinense,* the datil pepper can have quite a kick—the heat is roughly half that of the orange habanero, yet it has a similar citrus-zest flavor. The most common use of the datil pepper is in a sweet/spicy tomato-based BBQ sauce, but it is also sparingly added to the quintessential Floridian Minorcan dish, the pilau. However, the flavor of the datil stands out best, in our humble opinion, in a simple spicy vinegar. A large bottle is filled with datil peppers and white vinegar and the flavors are allowed to marry until the vinegar takes on a golden hue. It is the perfect accompaniment to any dish—try it in a Bloody Mary.

Kraig

filled with assorted condiments. Fortunately for us, it included a small jar of datil peppers in white vinegar—a simple, spicy condiment to accompany the food. We smiled at one another like old junkies who have just discovered that someone left a couple of joints in their midst.

"That's nothing—look at Johnny's collection above the counter." Bill pointed to a shelf that ran along near the top of the wall. On the shelf was a menagerie of one-liter liquor bottles—Crown Royal, Grey Goose, Wild Turkey—but each was filled with datil peppers cured in vinegar, each with a different mix of various and sundry seasonings.

"Some of those are over three years old—they just stay up there, marinating." Bill shook his head, amused at the size of Johnny's datil arsenal. "I have no idea what he's going to do with all of it." Bill sighed, as if he were observing a stockpile of weapons of mass destruction. Indeed, many of the bottles had taken on an opaque golden hue, as if they were radioactive. Before we could fully fathom how much damage that many cured datil peppers could do to the gastrointestinal systems of the world, our darkest thoughts were interrupted by the arrival of our food.

"Wow!" Kraig exclaimed, sizing up a fried pork chop placed in front of him that could make the state of Texas look teeny-weeny by comparison. "This is huge!"

"Needless to say, Johnny goes all out. Each morning, he makes a circuit through all the last remaining farm stands to buy what he needs for lunch that day," Bill explained as the rest of us dove into our lunches. Our plates were piled high with a formidable mix of southern flavors and textures. We set to sampling them as if it were our sacred duty as gastronauts. The only break in our silence was when Johnny came over to ask how everything was.

"This . . . this is extraordinary," Gary gushed. "I hate the word *authentic,* but you are doing something here with these greens and beans and per-lows that we simply don't have the chance to experience elsewhere in this country. I think you've found the pot at the end of the rainbow . . . and it looks like that rainbow ends in your own hometown!"

Johnny got serious for a second. "It does indeed. Hell, I literally grew up within blocks of this place." But then he caught himself sounding too devout and decided that he'd better lighten up. He had been leaning on the back of Bill's chair, but now he stood up all the way, gave a twist to his mustache, and reached up to the shelf above the cash register.

"Boys, if you can't remember my cooking when you get home, let me give you something that will burn it into your memories for good." His beefy hand grabbed a dusty decorator bottle of Chivas Regal that held enough datil-imbued vinegar to sink a battle fleet and then brought two more down, one for each of the gastronauts. Thanking Johnny for his generous gifts of aged vinegar, we asked him one last question: What's his secret for making the amazing Minorcan pilau that he had shared with us the night before? He demurred, apparently feeling that it was not his own *genius loci* but that of the entire community that made the pilau so special. Instead of answering us himself, he turned to the nearest table, where he had spotted an elderly woman who was a stalwart citizen of Hastings.

"Now, this lady here is a *real* Minorcan—I bet your mama made some of the best pilau, didn't she?" Johnny drew out the sound—*perlooow*—and his voice caught the attention of the elderly lady, who had been waiting for some friends to arrive, sipping a cup of coffee at the corner table. She looked up at Johnny and smiled a knowing, shy smile through her thin lips. She nodded.

This prompted Johnny to go on: "And I bet she started with onions, peppers, and tomatoes, didn't she?"

"Oh yes, she did. That's how my mama did it . . ."

"And she'd cook that down—for a long, long, long, long time; she'd cook it down until it was near black, didn't she?"

"Oh yes, she did."

"And not until it was nearly black did she even think about adding the rice."

"That's right."

"See, boys, *that's* how you make a real Minorcan pilau. You got to get the onions, tomatoes, and peppers nearly black before you start the rice. Long and slow—it's a process. Can take a full day to make it right. This lady grew up in a household where they did it right . . ."

As we meekly tried to express our gratitude to that elderly woman, we could see her beam with pride. Johnny knew he needn't say anything else, so he winked and waved good-bye. We cradled our whiskey bottles full of "sprinklin' vinegar" and headed out the door of Johnny's Kitchen to the Spice Ship. After thanking Bill Hamilton and dropping him off at his home on Crescent Beach, we flew off from the First Coast feeling that we, too, had glimpsed the pot at the end of the rainbow. That pot of gold was not just a bottle stuffed full of golden datil peppers. It was a place where a local cultural community takes such pride in its unique food traditions that it simply won't stand to let them disappear, climate change or no climate change. Even if the oceans do rise, as some scientists project that they will, it would not be surprising to learn that some Florida Crackers and Minorcans had saved their very highest ground for growing out an annual pepper patch. That's because datil peppers are not merely some commodity packed full of calories, vitamins, flavors, and pungency; they are cultural icons, signifiers, and artifacts, giving back to certain caring humans a sense of their own community identity, history, and individual self-worth.

## Datil Pepper Sauce

Nearly everyone along the First Coast has a couple of five-gallon plastic buckets in their backyards with datil bushes sprouting up to six feet high out of them. Those with more than a couple of buckets might sell the peppers to one of the small businesses in the area specializing in datil-based products, but for most people these backyard bushes are for their private use, filling dozens of Ball jars with sweet-hot, barbecue-like datil pepper sauce. Some make it smooth, others make it slightly chunky—and in that case it tends to be called "relish" by Minorcans and other St. Augustine locals, even though, technically speaking, it's still a sauce.

Each sauce varies in intensity and sweetness, but they all have roughly the same base: ketchup, vinegar, sugar, and of course datils. Of all the chiles we tasted in our journey, the datil was surely the one that stood out for its great balance of heat and depth, with just a hint of sweetness. The key to a good datil sauce is capturing this unique aspect rather than smothering it in ketchup.

The hottest part of a datil pepper, as with any chile, is the ribs—the white part inside that holds the seeds to the flesh of the pepper. You'll want to carefully remove all the ribs and seeds for this (and most) recipes.

Sealed tightly and refrigerated, this sauce can last for months. Properly canned, it can last for years. We consulted with food preservation guru Sherri Brooks Vinton, author of the recent book *Put 'Em Up*, for tips on canning this sauce, and she pointed out that the key is to make sure the pH is below 4.6—then you can use the simple hot-water bath method that your grandmother probably used. Simple pH test strips sold in gardening stores will give you a pretty good idea, but if you are going to do this sort of thing a lot and/or want to be certain, there are digital pH monitors available online for around a hundred dollars.

As with any of the hot chiles, keep these safety tips in mind: Those with sensitive skin should always wear protective gloves when handling chiles. Wash your hands both before and after chopping, and do not touch your eyes, nose, or—shall we say—other sensitive parts of your or anyone else's body after handling chiles. This is a lesson that we repeat frequently here, but that experience needs to teach only once.

5–7 datil peppers, stemmed, seeded, and minced (or to taste)

1 Vidalia (or other sweet) onion, peeled and minced

1 sweet red bell pepper, stemmed, seeded, and minced

3 cloves garlic, peeled and minced

2 cups cider vinegar

2 cups ketchup, preferably organic (avoid the stuff with high-fructose corn syrup in it)

2 tablespoons Worcestershire sauce

3 tablespoons sugar (or honey, or to taste)

Combine all ingredients in a medium (4-quart) stockpot, and place over medium-low heat. Stir frequently. When the mixture begins to simmer, reduce the heat to low and, still stirring frequently, cook down by at least one-third, or as much as one-half, according to taste. Let cool; then, if you want a smooth sauce, strain through a fine-mesh sieve or cheesecloth. This will reduce your yield significantly, though.

Store in airtight containers in the fridge, or can according to your equipment's instructions. *Yields about 3-4 cups when unstrained; this recipe doubles or even triples quite well.*

## Variations on Pilau

First things first. Kraig and Kurt were roundly chastised upon arrival at the fish camp because of their pronunciation of this dish. Whereas throughout most of the rest of the world it would be said just the way it's spelled, around these parts it is called PER-low.

Marjorie Kinnan Rawlings, the author best known for her Pulitzer Prize–winning book, *The Yearling*, was also a passionate cook and a chronicler of the "Cracker cuisine" of northeastern Florida. In her cookbook *Cross Creek Cookery*, she wrote of pilau, "No Florida church supper, no large rural gathering, is without it. It is blessed among dishes for such a purpose, or for a large family, for meat goes farther in pilau than prepared in any other way."

Variations on this dish exist anywhere rice is a staple. In Cajun country, a similar dish is called jambalaya. In Spain it is paella, in France pilaf, and in Turkey (thought to be its origin) it is called, in fact, pilau.

Ms. Rawlings details recipes for several different types, from chicken or pork to oxtail or coot liver and gizzard pilau (a coot is a waterfowl, similar to a duck). Her recipes, though, call for drastically overcooking the meat in most cases, by leaving it in with the rice as it cooks. This method may impart more flavor to the rice, but it will leave the meat or seafood a flavorless mash. Thus, we have taken a few liberties with Rawlings's view of tradition here.

Once the method is mastered, the possible variations are limited only by your imagination. The tricks are in not overcooking the meat and using an appropriate stock. Then of course there are the peppers. Almost any variety could be used, but those striving for authenticity should naturally stick with datils.

## A Note About the Rice

Most Crackers will use the ordinary white rice found in bags in any grocery store, and this works just fine. If you'd like to get a bit more flavor from your rice, consider using the somewhat quicker-cooking Thai jasmine rice. For a lot more nutritional value, look to long- or short-grain brown rice, both of which will take a lot longer to cook, but are worth it. Carolina Gold rice was used in Florida pilaus through the 1920s, and can be found once again. Spanish or Italian short-grain rices work well, too. Just please, no Minute Rice.

## Chicken or Pork Pilau

Rawlings's recipe essentially says to boil the chicken or pork in plain water until tender and then add salt and pepper and rice and cook until the rice is done, garnishing with chopped egg. She even calls for three times as much liquid as rice, rather than the customary two-to-one ratio. The result would be mushy and bland, to say the least. Here we suggest a few augmentations, such as using chicken stock, adding mirepoix (MEER-pwah, an aromatic blend of onion, carrot, and celery), and of course the datil chiles. A fresh herb never hurt anyone, either.

> 1 whole chicken, cut up into legs, thighs, breasts, and wings, carcass reserved
>     for stock; *or* four 1-inch-thick pork chops
> Salt and fresh-cracked black pepper to taste
> ¼ cup olive or peanut oil
> 1 large red onion, peeled and diced
> 2 medium carrots, peeled and diced
> 2 stalks celery, diced
> 2 cloves garlic, peeled and sliced paper-thin
> 2–4 datil peppers (or to taste), minced
> 1 bay leaf
> 2 cups rice (see the note, above)

4 cups chicken stock–homemade is preferred, but the low-sodium store-
bought is okay
2 hard-boiled eggs, peeled and chopped (for garnish)
2 tablespoons chopped fresh parsley (for garnish)

Wash the chicken or pork under cold running water and pat dry
with paper towels. Season liberally with salt and pepper and
set aside.

Heat a large (8-quart) stockpot over medium heat, then add
the oil, followed by some of the chicken or pork. Do not crowd
the pan–this can be done in two or three batches. Brown the
meat on all sides, then remove to a plate and set aside. The
meat is not fully cooked yet, but it will be–see below.

In the same pan, with the remaining oil and drippings from
the cooked meat, combine the onion, carrot, celery, garlic,
peppers, and bay leaf. Sauté, stirring frequently, until the vegetables are tender but not browned. Add the rice and continue
to sauté a few minutes more, until the rice becomes somewhat
translucent. Add the chicken stock and reduce the heat to low.
Stir thoroughly once more, then cover and cook until the liquid
is absorbed. The time here varies according to the type of rice
used, but it is usually about 20 to 25 minutes for white rices, and
40 to 45 minutes for brown and Carolina Gold rices.

### To Finish the Meat

There are two ways to cook the meat the rest of the way
through here. One is to simply pop it into a 350°F oven for
about 10 to 12 minutes and then serve it on top of the rice.
With this method you'll get sweeter, more caramelized meat.
The other is to reintroduce the chicken or pork into the pot
with the cooking rice about 8 to 10 minutes before it finishes
absorbing the stock. Make sure to get it fully submerged if
you go this route.

## Another Option

Depending on how many people you want to serve, it might be worthwhile to dice the cooked pork chops or pull the chicken from the bones with a fork and mix this into the rice. This, as Ms. Rawlings points out, will stretch the meat further.

Garnish with the chopped egg and parsley, and serve immediately. *Serves 4–8.*

## Shrimp Pilau

Rawlings offers two totally different versions of shrimp pilau, one essentially following the same sort of method (boil the heck out of it) as her chicken recipe. The other has the rice cooked separately and sautés the rest of the ingredients, to be mixed together at service. The latter is at least more palatable than the former, again in order to avoid overcooking the shrimp (an all-too-common culinary sin). It is important to note that, amid the strong ethnic Minorcan population in the area, a shrimp pilau is anathema, and would be shunned as inauthentic. Sure is tasty, though.

And so the recipe below uses a similar method to the one above, though the ingredients are a little different.

2 cups fresh shrimp, peeled and deveined (leaving the tail on is optional)
¼ cup rendered fatback or bacon fat (or as needed)
Salt and fresh-cracked black pepper to taste
1 large red onion, peeled and diced
2 medium carrots, peeled and diced
2 stalks celery, diced
2 cloves garlic, peeled and sliced paper-thin
2 ripe tomatoes, peeled, seeded, and diced
2–4 datil peppers (or to taste), minced
1 bay leaf
2 cups rice (see note for preceeding recipe)
4 cups shrimp or fish stock
1 cup sliced fresh okra
½ cup all-purpose flour, seasoned with salt and white pepper
2 tablespoons butter
Lemon wedges (for garnish)

Whether you leave the tails on or not, a nice presentation of the shrimp is to slice them lengthwise down the middle—clean through if there's no tail, or leaving the two sides of the shrimp attached at the tail if there is one. The latter is more appealing visually, but some folks prefer to avoid the mild hassle of removing the tail when they eat. Either way, rinse them and thoroughly pat them dry with a paper towel before cooking.

In a large (8-quart) stockpot, heat the rendered fat over medium-high heat. Add the shrimp, 1/2 to 2/3 cup at a time so as not to crowd the pan. Season lightly with salt and pepper. Sauté each batch, stirring frequently, until pink and firm, probably less than 2 minutes per batch. Remove and set aside on clean paper towels. Repeat until all the shrimp are cooked.

In the same stockpot, adding a bit more pork fat if needed, combine the onion, carrots, celery, garlic, tomatoes, peppers, and bay leaf. Reduce the heat to medium and sauté, stirring frequently, until the vegetables are tender but not browned. Add the rice and continue to sauté a few minutes more, until the rice becomes somewhat translucent. Add the shrimp or fish stock and reduce the heat to low. Stir thoroughly once more, then cover and cook until the liquid is absorbed. The time here varies according to the type of rice, but it is usually about 20 to 25 minutes for white rices, and 40 to 45 minutes for brown rices.

While the rice cooks, dredge the okra in the seasoned flour and fry until browned in small batches in butter, in a skillet over medium heat. Set aside on clean paper towels.

When the rice is finished, taste for salt and pepper, adjust if needed, stir in the shrimp, and serve immediately, garnished with the fried okra and lemon wedges. *Serves 4–8.*

# CHAPTER THREE

# Hard Times and Habaneros in the Yucatán

**BY THE TIME** the three gastronauts had reunited at the Spice Ship in Mérida, Mexico, we realized we would be storm-chasing a wild spirit named Ida for the next few weeks. Hurricane Ida was the biggest twister during the relatively tranquil storm season of 2009, and she was generating quite a bit of banter on the Weather Channel. However, by the time the Spice Ship crossed her tracks, Ida was no longer pelting rain down upon the Yucatán Peninsula, having slid north into the Gulf of Mexico. She had nevertheless left quite a bit of damage in her wake, leaving about forty thousand people homeless on her path from Nicaragua northward. As Ida moved from the Yucatán toward the Gulf Coast of the United States, she was downgraded to a tropical storm, one that looked like it might peter out altogether.

It did not. Instead, Ida gained strength and ravaged the Gulf Coast, especially the Florida Panhandle, and then joined forces with a nor'easter to rage up the Atlantic seaboard. In New York and New England, tens of thousands of families were left without power, and thousands had to temporarily leave their homes. In Virginia alone, the damage from the storm was estimated at thirty-nine million dollars.

While we missed Ida in her fury, we were given a chance to see how farmers and their chile crops must inevitably deal with the aftermath of any major hurricanes. We kept on having to remind ourselves and the farmers we spoke with that hurricanes are not *caused* by global warming, though the severity and frequency of certain kinds of tropical storms seem to be heightened by warming trends in certain regions. No scientist would argue that a particular hurricane is *evidence* of global climate change per se, but by documenting the ecological, agricultural, and cultural chaos stirred up by hurricanes, we are given a window into the future, where our communities may have to deal with greater climatic unpredictability on a more frequent basis.

In the nine days preceding our visit to habanero chile farmers on the peninsula, Ida had dropped some nine inches on Yucatecan fields and dooryard gardens—about a quarter of the year's rainfall in one event— devouring beaches and leaving many windfalls in its wake.

Of course, all this force prompted comparisons between Hurricane Ida and the historic Hurricane Gilbert, a massive storm that had wreaked so much havoc in 1988, it had literally restructured how Mayan agriculture was practiced in some regions. Gilbert wiped out an entire year's worth of crops, and the subsequent year's crops were plagued by high levels of pests, which were thought to have been caused by the lack of bird habitat after Gilbert, or to be an insect population boom caused by their feasting on all the ruined crops in the fields. Although Ida's winds and disruptions to wildlife were initially not as powerful as Gilbert's, the ripple effects had just begun. And so we hightailed it out of Mérida to see what we could see from the windows of the Spice Ship. The first place where we got a good look at the hurricane's "vapor trails" was in the sleepy beach town of Progreso on the northern Yucatán coast.

We first approached Progreso before dusk, when the sky was still packed with churning masses of grayish clouds. Some had a sickly yellow tinge to them, while others, off in the distance, were charcoal gray and still shedding rain. Progreso's streets had standing water up over the curbs to the level of the sidewalks, even though most of the runoff had been shed into backwater lagoons that sat behind the barrier island forming Progreso's prime beachfront property.

The lagoons edging Progreso were filled to the brim, their turbid waters spilling over into adjacent scrublands and swelling to the highest levels that folks had seen in recent years. If you were skeptical of the veracity of the memories among Progreso's human occupants regarding the relative severity of this storm, you could take a hint from the flocks of flamingos. They appeared to be profoundly agitated, as if the floods that followed in Ida's wake had rudely displaced them. Flocks of eight to twelve flamingos flitted from spot to spot, testing to see how high the water came up their stilt legs. If the water was too deep for them to get their beaks down near the bottom to feed, they moved on once more. The water was still too deep and too churned up with mud for them to feed successfully pretty much anywhere, so the flamingos set off again and again, fleeing from one patch of floodwaters to another. It was hard for us not to anthropomorphize about birds that were nearly our own size. We concluded that these were flamingos frustrated by their lack of bigger beaks. They flapped around listlessly, as if suffering from post-hurricane stress.

After cruising around Progreso making our quick assessment of the hurricane's aftermath, we brought the Spice Ship to a halt in the neighboring town of Chelem at the beach house of Nancy and Jeff Gerlach. Years ago, Nancy had helped found *Chile Pepper* magazine with our friend and mentor Dave DeWitt, with whom she had also coauthored *Habanero* and *The Spicy Food Lover's Bible*. She was the perfect person to orient us for our explorations. Nancy and her husband, Jeff, warmly greeted us at the door of their two-story beach bungalow. They immediately assured us that they would have plenty of habanero stories to tell us after a while, but as soon as we came in through their front door, they escorted us straight through the house and out their back door. It seemed like sort of a Marx Brothers routine, going in one door and out the other. But for once—unlike Groucho, Chico, and Harpo—the three gastronauts were obedient guests. Upon reaching the back patio, we realized why Jeff and Nancy had led us to the waterfront: The ocean was literally below our feet. There, on the ocean side of the house, they wanted us to see just how much sand Hurricane Ida had robbed from the Yucatán Peninsula over the previous week.

"Our neighbors tell us that they used to have enough space in front of homes to play *fútbol* before they hit the upper tide line. Now look at it—or what's left of it . . ." Jeff sighed, pointing down to some black bags floating in the shallows about ten yards out from their porch. Wearing a Hawaiian shirt, khaki shorts, and sandals, he was in a dark mood that clashed with his sunny beach wear.

Nancy chimed in. She could be short-winded, and was often slow to pipe up, but unerringly thoughtful and precise in whatever she offered. She pointed to some big black, shiny blobs bouncing around in the surf just a few yards out from where we stood.

"We call those storm-buffering bags 'whales,' but the storm surge was so massive this time that they didn't do us much good. We don't think we'll permanently lose the beach in front of us here, but that's frankly what all our neighbors are now worried about. This beach is about as small as they've ever seen it . . . And they say that over at Cancún it's even worse . . . they've lost thousands of tons of sand from their beaches this week, and, believe me, beaches are their bread and butter . . ."

We went back into the Gerlachs' living room but kept the doors open, letting the salty sea breeze waft over us. Inland, it had been sweltering, but now, as the sun moved toward the water, it was cooling off nicely. Jeff and Nancy began to bring a raft of habanero paraphernalia off their shelves—various salsas, vinegars, books, seeds, and encapsulated powders of roasted, dried, and ground habanero peppers.

"You may not believe this," Jeff began hesitantly, with obvious humility, "but while Nancy was writing about the history of habaneros, this stuff kind of saved my life. I've had really bad rheumatoid arthritis over the last few years—that's one reason why we wanted to move down here, away from the cold in the mountains of northern New Mexico. Some days that we lived up there, the arthritis would just cramp me up. In fact, I'd get so stove up I could hardly do anything . . ."

Jeff paused and looked over to Nancy as if acknowledging how

hard that time had been for them, and then went on. "Well then, in
her research, Nancy encountered these studies suggesting that chile
consumption could improve blood circulation. So I found some dried
habanero powder, started putting it in vitamin capsules, and pretty
soon my arthritic symptoms were not merely reduced, they were just
plain gone.

"Now, you might want to attribute the improvement of my condition to other factors, like moving down here into a different climate
. . . But when we first arrived here, we were so busy that I forgot to
take any of the capsules for the first couple of weeks. My arthritic
condition reverted to what it had been, until I started taking those
blasted capsules again. Now I'm hooked on them, I'm feeling so good,
but I'm having trouble finding enough dried ground habanero chile
powder to keep me going. As you know, they don't usually dry them
around here; they use them fresh. So I can't always find dried habanero powder. It's not a big market, I suppose. What I'm suggesting is
that, while you boys are out and about, if you come across anyone
selling the powder, give me a heads-up!"

We agreed we'd keep a lookout for Jeff and we were sent off, armed
with suggestions on foods to try and places to go.

Out into the field we went, but not until we went to market first. We
headed to the municipal market in Mérida, where we wanted to see just
how habaneros have been traditionally prepared, marketed, and sold to
home-style cooks as well as restaurant chefs. We trudged through the
mud from the recent rains, but thanks to a tin roof towering above the
market stalls, most of the *mercado's* stalls had survived the hurricane's
winds and rains with no ill effects. We wandered a maze of narrow
aisles, each sided by fruit, vegetable, or spice stands loaded with dozens
of fragrant items.

Less than a minute inside the market, we were led to the booth of
La Rosita's Expendio de Condimentos Yucateca, with a seventy-five-
year history of selling spices, including peppers. Below Rosita's banner
was a smaller sign proclaiming CHILE HABANERO MOLIDO—just the stuff
that Jeff Gerlach needed. While buying a couple of baby-food jars of

the fiery powder to save for Jeff, we became intrigued by the many spice mixtures or *recados* being sold by Rosita's family and the other vendors nearby.

You can't really understand the distinctive roots of Yucatecan food traditions until you understand *recados.* Yucatecan food is an amalgam of Mayan, Spanish, Caribbean, and more recent European and Middle Eastern influence. One example of this influence is found in the now omnipresent *tacos al pastor*—spit-roasted spiced meats eaten on a flour tortilla with a bit of pineapple. The spit-roasting is reminiscent of a gyro or shwarma—the Middle Eastern influence is clear here, and *tacos al pastor* can in fact be traced back to Lebanese immigrants. Another example of culinary European–Mexican hybridization is reflected in the use of the *recados,* a local spice mixture that epitomizes Yucatecan culinary history. That word is an archaic Spanish term for "keepsake" or "good keeper."

"My guess is that these spice mixtures are much like the ones found in Andalucía right before the Spanish Inquisition," Gary explained to Kurt, "with the exception that none of them had any chile pepper powder in them back then. But when Andalucía's Moslems and Jews fled to Yucatán and Veracruz, they not only brought with them the *ras el-hanout* ["shopkeeper's choice"] mix of spices, but particular ingredients came with them as well. Look at this one—it's a *recado para escabeche.* It's got black pepper, cinnamon, garlic, cumin, and laurel from the Old World—just like many *baharat* mixtures of the Moors—and allspice as well as Mexican oregano from the New . . ."

*"Escabeche?"* Kurt asked. His mother happened to be a talented lexicographer of food terms and their diffusion around the world; that interest had obviously rubbed off. "Same root as *ceviche,* right? They cook fish or fowl in vinegar mixed with spices such as cumin, cinnamon, ginger . . ."

"Their linguistic roots, curiously enough, run back to *al-sikbaj,* an Arabic term for a cold dish that has been 'cooked' in vinegar."

"But do any of these *recados* now have habaneros in them?" Kurt inquired.

"I dunno." Gary paused. "Let's ask vendors at a couple of different booths . . . each of them may prepare a slightly different version of a *recado* sold by the same name." We wandered off down the narrow aisles past huge piles of red, black, ash-gray, brown, and orange pastes.

We spotted a short, distinguished-looking man standing behind high heaps of spice pastes. After listening to our question, he grinned and shrugged. "Well, you can certainly add a little habanero powder to my *recado negro,* but not many of my customers want that," this elderly Mayan man explained. "I roast and scorch other, more mild chiles for my base. So if you want something hotter, I'll sell you some habanero to make it more *picante* . . ."

Across the aisle, a younger, more opportunistic vendor smirked. "If you want habanero in it, I will put it in for you. Some of my other customers want it that way, and you know, I'll put in whatever the customer wants . . ."

"I first decide if the *recado* is balanced, and that's what matters," said another. "If the habanero is too strong, it overwhelms everything else. If it's a mild one that gives the whole mixture more flavor, I'll put a little in, but I have to be careful."

It was clear that the criteria for adding habaneros to *recados* were still evolving, just as *recados* themselves may have evolved from *baharat* spice mixtures such as *ras el-hanout, zaatar, masala,* and *sellou* from the Old World, and prehistoric chile-and-chocolate mole from the New World. There are *recados* for traditional Mayan dishes like *cochinita pibil,* the famous slow-roasted pork dish, which contains mostly New World ingredients (achiote, allspice, Mexican oregano), but also some Old World ones like cumin, peppercorns, and garlic. Habaneros, some food historians surmise, may not have entered into *recado* mixtures until just prior to the Mexican Revolution, when they were presumably transported up ancient trade routes from Central and South America, or perhaps from the Caribbean. Unlike most other chile pepper varieties grown on the peninsula, they have no Mayan name of their own, a possible indicator of their relatively recent adoption in the Yucatán. While many traditional varieties of chiles carry Mayan names (*x'catic, sukurre*), the habanero has a Spanish name. And yet, while they are slowly finding their way into more *recado* spice mixtures, habaneros are already a mainstay in salsas, fish, and tamale-like dishes of the Maya, some of which carry Mayan names. The fiery salsa that is found at local taco and *salbute* vendors is called the dog's-nose salsa—*xnipek*—and features the habanero with sour orange and thinly sliced onions.

Habaneros not only are considered a traditional Yucatecan food but have been blessed with an official "denomination of origin" to demar-cate the link between habaneros, Mayan culture, and Yucatecan places. The denomination of origin is a Protected Designation of Origin or PDO, something that is quite common in European Union coun-tries—for instance, it is how Appellation d'Origine Contrôlée works in France with respect to wines and cheeses. In Mexico it is fairly new, but Mexico has already protected such important culinary traditions as tequila from Jalisco, mescal from Oaxaca, and vanilla from Papantla. The habanero is the first PDO chile in Mexico, linking the Yucatán to the habanero forever.

And yet it was clear that such links stretch and shift. Many of the Mayans with whom we spoke hinted that the habanero's status is constantly changing in their Yucatecan cuisine, and that it will continue to do so.

Of course, one of the other shifts that Yucatecans bear witness to is shifting weather patterns. Whether or not all such shifts are linked to global climate change, they have been evident to some of the Yucatán's farmers, foragers, and naturalists for at least two decades.

To gain a sense of the severity of those shifts to date, and those projected to occur in the future, Kraig had arranged for us to visit scien-tists at the Centro de Investigación Científica de Yucatán, who had ongo-ing research projects on climate change in the peninsula. Their campus sits in the midst of a tropical botanical garden begun some twenty years ago on the edge of Mérida. Today its surroundings have been all but swallowed up by suburbs, and the campus itself is like a wild island in an urban sea. There one of the garden's founders, biologist Roger Orellana

# Habanero

## (Capsicum chinense)

There would seem to be much confusion to clear up about the habanero, one of the most pungent of all peppers.

*Capsicum chinense,* from what little we know, first evolved and was domesticated in the Amazon basin and found its way to the Caribbean. It's likely that the first chile pepper Columbus bit into (which was called *ají* by the Taíno Indians) was a *Capsicum chinense.* Columbus and his men are to thank for the confusing Spanish and Portuguese homograph linking black pepper–*pimenta* (*Piper nigrum*)–and chile pepper, which he first called *pimenta* (in Mexico, the word *chile* is used). This marking reversal is reflected in the way in which North American English uses *pepper* for both foods.

Such linguistic ambivalences are rife throughout the habanero origin story. For instance, it was assumed that *habanero* is a derivative from *Habana*–suggesting that perhaps the pepper has origins in Cuba. A quick glance at Cuban food will tell you what subsequent genetic tests have concluded–the origin of the species lies within the Amazon basin, with an early migration to Central America and the Caribbean. Another popular misconception is that *habanero* refers to the entire species. Not exactly. The name refers to a specific pod type–the distinguishing characteristics of the chile fruit–a type of horticultural division within pepper species. Habanero belongs to the same species as the Florida datil, the Caribbean Scotch bonnets, and the recently "discovered" Bhut Jolokia–the hottest pepper ever measured.

The habanero is currently associated with the Yucatán Peninsula, but we don't know the date of its introduction there. Although there is ample evidence of pre-Colombian chile consumption by the Maya in various drinks and foods described by early ethnographers, the varieties and types they used are unknown.

Linguistic evidence points to a later introduction, as the habanero has a Spanish-derived name, whereas other chiles grown on the Yucatán Peninsula have Mayan names–*x'catic, sukurre, maax-ik.* At the same time, the most traditional and ubiquitous habanero salsa has a Mayan moniker–*xnipek,* dog's-nose salsa.

Lanza, took us on narrow pathways through the small jungle to see some experiments that had tried to simulate the effects of temperature and carbon dioxide enrichment on habanero growth and health.

Roger was enthusiastic about his student René Garruña's habanero experiments, but at the same time he looked weary. He had just completed a multiyear project to be released that week—the *Atlas*

The habanero, much like most pepper plants, cuts quite a figure in the field. It is broader-leafed than other species, and its brightly colored fruits come in oranges and reds–the warning colors of nature–to fore-shadow the heat inside.

The lantern-shaped fruit itself isn't very fleshy, but it has a distinct aroma, a citrus/acidic smell. Given the relatively recent interest in the habanero, there have been releases of improved varieties, which tend to be yellow-orange when mature. In contrast, the local land races tend to be red upon reaching maturity.

The habanero has developed into quite a big business, and not just for local consum-ers. Due to the various properties of the pepper, above all its extreme pungency, there are a number of industrial and culi-nary consumers on a global level. In 2007, the Yucatán produced about four thousand tons of habaneros, of which 20 percent was exported to the United States and Japan.

Enter China. The Chinese are already the world's largest group of producers (and consumers) of chiles, but recently they have been growing and competing with Mexican growers on the global market. To add insult to injury, they are using the same varieties of chiles that Mexicans grow and use–often selling them at lower prices. It is said that the majority of the *chile del arbol* in Mexico–the most common chile used in taco stand salsas–now comes from China. In response, Mexico has taken the unique step of establishing a denomination of origin for habaneros from the Yucatán. The denomina-tion of origin is a European concept. The idea is to protect certain singular goods that are products of their relationship with a place–in other words, protecting the *terroir* as a brand. *Jamón ibérico* or Rioja, for instance, can only come from certain regions in Spain; Mexico has copied this type of distinction and protected the most Mexican of beverages, tequila. Now it has extended this protection to habaneros, recognizing that the unique relationship among the Yucatán peninsula, the people, and the habanero is worth more than cheap Chinese imitations.

Kraig

*of Scenarios for Climate Change on the Peninsula of Yucatán.* In the lap-sized atlas, Roger and half a dozen of his colleagues mapped shifting zones of vulnerability to heightened annual temperatures, torren-tial rainfalls, midsummer droughts, and other conditions under four possible scenarios of severity for the year 2020. They then speculated about how their forecasts could be used as a tool to mitigate future impacts on corn cultivation, beekeeping, spice production, and the generation of hydropower, and to assess the risk of wildfires on the peninsula. Although most of the scenarios gave him pause, Roger was also frank about what the ninety-six color maps in the atlas could *not* capture.

"The problem with forecasting climate change," he told us, "is the very unpredictability of extreme phenomena, such as the hurricane which just passed through. I can document changes in the frequency of hurricanes and tropical storms, but really can't predict how intense their winds or rains might be, or how they will affect crops and other plants. Our models are better at predicting incremental change . . . For instance, we know that if we increase $CO_2$, it is likely to increase temperatures as well. But while $CO_2$ enrichment may stimulate growth in some plants, if you increase temperatures past a point, the system just may short out, so to speak."

Roger, like Mark Barnes in Florida, had a face which featured vertical furrows between his brows, which deepened every time he expounded on a topic. These furrows looked like they had been carved out over time, during which Roger had pondered the implications embedded in every multicolored map in his atlas night after night.

"The same dilemma is true whenever we try to deal with complex phenomena. Right now, we know of examples of climatic impacts, but we still cannot predict them very well. Let me give you an ecological example from the peninsula here, found by my colleagues at the University of Mérida. We have already reported that the phenologies—you know, flowering and fruiting times of plants—are shifting in time. The flowers are blooming earlier, and the insect pollinators that visit the flowers are not all ready for that. Some of the insects are typically eaten by migratory birds like Wilson's warbler, but it is not arriving here in time for the shifted phenologies, and so they are starving or dying.

"Are food chains based on plants vulnerable to such shifts? We simply don't know, we just don't know." Roger sighed. But then he recalled something else.

"Most flowers on chile plants in the tropics are pollinated by tiny sweat bees—you may already know that. But what we don't know is if the hatching and emergence times for sweat bees are shifting, or if the same bees form much of the diet for migratory birds when they come across the peninsula . . ."

We had come out of the cool shade of the botanical garden's forest-like canopy and were entering the hothouses where Roger and René had programmed growth chambers to emulate some of the scenarios Roger's atlas had modeled. There we saw our first habanero plants "in the field," if you will.

The field, in this case, was a set of eight-foot-tall growth chambers nested within the larger greenhouse. There, under double cover, habaneros were grown in pots with light, temperature, and carbon dioxide maintained at particular levels. Each growth chamber's environment had been programmed to a different temperature setting—86, 95, or 104 degrees Fahrenheit—and to one of two carbon dioxide levels—one near the current atmospheric conditions (about 380 parts per million), and one double that.

Roger opened the door and the four of us piled inside one of the chambers, an experimental "field" that was already filled with potted plants, instruments, and $CO_2$ emitters that looked like large nozzles. It was easy to feel claustrophobic in here. A few minutes ago we had stood under the large canopy of the forest, and now we were inside the much smaller glass cubes with their orange, green, and cream-colored habanero fruit, and the various and sundry gadgets filling up every last little bit of space.

But we soon acclimated ourselves to the cramped quarters, and we remained inside as Roger explained to us the preliminary experimental results that he and René had generated. It appeared that the habanero plants responded favorably to increased levels of $CO_2$, as long as the threshold point of photosynthetic saturation was not reached. But as Roger had hinted earlier, and now reiterated, "If you get $CO_2$ and temperature too high, it's the biological equivalent of becoming flammable. Metabolically, the plant can no longer function . . . But we can't easily predict from these growth chambers where the tipping point will be under true field conditions."

We were starting to pick up a consistent theme from Roger's explanations. Most plants, including chile peppers, will respond favorably to increased levels of $CO_2$, which allows them to grow faster, but each of them benefits only to a certain point—and not taking into account the mitigating factor of simultaneously increasing temperatures. Whether we consider the current computer models or data from experiments done in controlled environments, we can control one or two variables and can to some extent predict the consequences of those causal factors alone, but *both* nature and agriculture are much more complex than that. Roger was a seasoned scientist, one with enough experience to have been humbled by just how little we can reasonably predict of the workings of nature by altering just one or two variables at a time. His ultimate strategy for understanding climatic change effects on habaneros was not *reductionist* but rather *synthetic*. He sought to build a web of knowledge from various strands of experiments and modeled scenarios so that he and René might ultimately catch a little more truth in their predictions. It was an iterative process, slow but grounded in a dynamic sense of causes and effects.

Just as we came out of the greenhouses, Roger spotted René on the trail ahead of us. He called out, and a smiling, curly-headed, muscular student turned toward us and came back down the trail to meet us. It was clear he had agrarian roots and was not a doom-and-gloomer, a cynic set on making dire predictions about habaneros going to hell in a handbasket. What motivated a former agronomist to come back to graduate school to assess the effects of accelerated climate change on the humble habanero?

"For several years, I had the opportunity to work with pepper growers all over the peninsula. They are my friends . . . Well, they are like family," Rene stammered, his eyes gazing out into the tropical garden. And then, he simply added one more phrase to his explanation.

"I am looking into their future."

• • •

The next day, another friend of Kraig's had promised to take us out to meet such farmers, not in the market, not in the growth chamber, but in the field.

"I told Jorge that we want to see all scales of habanero production, from the Mayan dooryard garden to the farm designed for commercial production of peppers to be exported to the US, Korea, and Japan. I think Jorge's our man for this task. He works for INIFAP, the Mexican agricultural research program, but he's widely traveled and has good personal relationships with farmers all over the place. I met him at a chile research conference a couple years ago and we hit it off."

Jorge Berny appeared in our hotel lobby in Mérida at about dawn that morning, ready to take us out into some of the very areas that Roger's atlas suggested might be most vulnerable in the near future to short-term climate change. But what we soon heard from the farmers themselves was that they have already been experiencing such vulnerability for more than two decades.

Our next stop was at INIFAP's own demonstration farm, the Uxmal Agricultural Experiment Station, which had recently hosted a field day as part of a conference for chile breeders, pathologists, and agronomists from all over the world. The fields were extremely well kept and nearly free of weeds, but the recent rains from Hurricane Ida had turned their furrows into muddy alleys. We rolled up the cuffs of our jeans and started our way down the rows where several traditional heirloom varieties as well as improved varieties of habaneros grew. It didn't take us long to accumulate several inches of wet red clay on our heels and soles. With more clay glomming onto us with every step, by the time we had trudged fifty yards through the muddy fields, it looked as if we were wearing platform shoes.

The rains had not just turned the fields into a mud bath, but had aggravated the severity of leaf symptoms of viral infections and insect infestations. Nearly every kind of chile we passed had a stunted curly top of miniaturized, bonsai-like distorted and curled foliage, or yellowed, limp-longing leaves, or the telltale signs of leaf miners feeding along the veins. In short, we were passing through a sick ward, looking to see if there were signs of resistance anywhere among the troops of peppers.

Fortunately, there was indeed evidence that a few kinds of heirloom habaneros did have genetic resistance to a particularly troublesome strain of Huasteco mosaic virus. Eight years before, at this very experimental station, agronomists such as Jorge had assembled many different collections of heirloom habanero varieties traditionally grown among the Maya and their *mestizo* neighbors. The seeds of these collections were germinated and then grown out where they could be specifically inoculated with the gemni-virus that caused the leaf diseases first noticed in Mexico in the fields of the Huastec Mayan farmers to the north of the Yucatán Peninsula.

To the agronomists' surprise, all habaneros were not born equal before the gemni-virus gods. Some were wimps that died as soon as they were infected. Others could be infected by the gemni-virus but tolerated its presence without much loss of pepper yields, while a few others were entirely resistant and seemed to repel the virus. Thus, genetic variation with habanero peppers was not simply limited to traits such as fruit color, flavor, size, shape, or sizzle; it mattered in terms of their capacity to survive all manner of changing weather patterns, pests, and diseases.

Jorge took us down one row where we encountered an improved variety of habanero that was being aggressively marketed by Seminis, a seed company purchased by Monsanto a few years back. The fear among genetic conservationists was that a single improved habanero variety—if marketed far and wide on the peninsula—might usurp the field space now occupied by dozens of different heirloom strains, causing the loss of diversity that might be needed for shaking off another newly introduced gemni-virus. But as we saw, the improved variety itself had its own problems with one of the many gemni-virus strains already on the peninsula. It was looking a little subdued.

We cruised another fifteen minutes back through the hurricane-clipped dwarf rain forest to what you might call a commercial-scale habanero farm on the edge of a village named Muna. Through most of the year, the farm was worked only by a husband-and-wife team with the occasional help of a few of their friends. When it came time to harvest, a truckload of migrant workers arrived, so that they could harvest the peppers just as they ripened. They grew several heirloom variants of habaneros in addition to three other peppers and a few other vegetable crops. But habaneros were the bread and butter for Rogelio Narvaez Dominguez and Guadalupe Isabel Vargas Ku.

Rogelio and Guadalupe Isabel were not your stereotypical farmers. Both were rather rotund and deeply bronzed by the sun. They were casually dressed in floppy beach hats, T-shirts, shorts, and sandals, as if their doctor had just told them to go out and get some exercise every day. But their exercise—both physical and mental—was how to keep enough habaneros alive to keep themselves alive. The increasingly frequent sweep of hurricanes through their half dozen hectares of pepper fields was one of their most daunting challenges.

Rogelio tried to explain in his Mayan-accented Spanish. "It's not just the damage that the hurricanes immediately do, but what comes after. Once *el Huracán Gilberto* had come through here, drenching our fields, we began to see diseases on the pepper we had not seen before. They say that Gilberto was so big and powerful that he picked up some viruses in Africa and they landed over here. I don't know where they came from really, but suddenly they were here on our habaneros."

Rogelio frowned, caught his breath, then went on: "The agronomists call them gemni-viruses. Some curl the leaves of our chiles or make spots on them, but mostly the yield of chiles goes down if they come and stay. So we work hard to keep the plants healthy so the habaneros can still be harvested."

Underneath those floppy beach hats were some active minds that had chosen not to fall victim to any chile infirmities that might degrade their own well-being and income-generating capacity. They had established their own pepper selection program, noting plants that appeared to be disease-free with good-quality fruits. Some heirlooms did better than others, and so they saved the seeds of those for future planting and increase. They also monitored diseases and insects with the help of Jorge Berny and other agronomists so that they would have an early warning if an outbreak emerged. And they used integrated pest management to reduce the severity of such outbreaks as they came on. As we talked, it was clear that Rogelio and Guadalupe Isabel had learned to roll with the flow. They were not wealthy and they worked hard all season long, but when things were going well, they did get a fair return on their investments and their sweat equity.

Still, they admitted, there were many pressures beyond their control. The price of habaneros goes up and down, depending on market demand in faraway places like Japan and Korea. Viruses and weeds can come in from anywhere, as they already have, apparently, from Africa. And it seemed to them that giant multinational companies had great influence on the cost of pesticides and fertilizers.

The way they talked about the prospects for their farm reminded us a bit of high-stakes poker players, commercial salmon fishermen, or venture capitalists. They wore the risks they dealt with every day right on their shirtsleeves. Uncertainty never went away. At most, they merely took a forty-minute break from their normal risk taking while we stood with them in the mud between pepper plants and speculated about the future of habaneros.

From Muna, we piloted the Spice Ship on to one of the larger traditional Maya market towns, called Oxkkutzcab. Oh, those Yucatecan *mercados*! It was hard not to be dazzled by all the diversity we found there, even in a medium-sized Mayan pueblo. At least five kinds of peppers were featured in a chaos of colors and shapes: habaneros, jalapeños, cayennes, anchos, and güeros. Then there were the tomatoes—from egg-shaped to spherical—and the chayotes, epazotes, chaya greens, and beans. The fragrances of tropical fruits, even in late fall, were enough to leave us weak in the knees: papayas and melons, limes and pineapples, zapotes and avocados, dragon fruit and custard apples. Other places in the market featured turkeys and chickens ready for plucking, corn and bean pods ready for shucking, allspice and coffee beans ready for grinding.

If we looked at these foods all together—seeds, breeds, and fruits; eggs, cheeses, and spices—it seemed like an unsinkable diversity and abundance of foodstuffs had reached the Mayan kitchen. But if we looked at them one at a time, as we had been doing for the various place-based heirloom peppers scattered around the continent, each one seemed to have its own vulnerability. A pepper plant riddled by thrips, covered in aphids, or deformed by curly-top was not a pretty sight to see.

Yet most consumers never see these problems. We are separated by where our food comes from, our view obfuscated by the bright fluorescent lights of our supermarket. The majority of the Yucatecan consumers get to select from the many gems that somehow made it out of the Mayan *milpa* fieldscape unscathed. We gain a false sense of food security if we never make it into the field, orchard, or dooryard garden where little battles between climate, soils, and crops go on day in and day out, from dawn until the wee hours of the night.

Jorge Berny gave us several options for rounding out our day. We opted to see a traditional Mayan orchard-garden where habaneros were grown, although it was many miles away. Jorge selected the Mayan village of Chacsinkin as our last field stop before night fell on the peninsula.

When we arrived in Chacsinkin, we immediately felt a sense of relief: It appeared as though traditional rural Mayan life was proceeding, uninterrupted, as it had for hundreds of years. The thatch-roofed houses were well kept, and they were surrounded by dooryard gardens containing many medicinal, edible, and fiber-bearing species of plants. Flocks of native turkeys wandered around the yards, gobbling up spilled grains, beans, or greens. Hedges with brilliantly red achiote berries on large seed heads added flames of color against the muted beiges and browns of adobe walls. Banana and papaya plants were everywhere.

But Idelfonso Yah Alcocer, our Mayan host, had some bad news for us: Hurricane Ida had dumped so much rain on these parts that he would not be able to take us back to his *milpa*.

"Not even with the Spice Ship's four-wheel drive?" we asked him.

"No, it's a swamp back there," Idelfonso replied, waving his hand in the direction of the *milpa*. "We'll get out of one mud hole and then get trapped in another . . ."

"Not even if we go there on foot?"

Idelfonso shook his head. "It's a few kilometers' hike on a dry day, but there are so many new pools from the rain that we wouldn't be able to walk straight there . . . And besides, we'd all look like mud balls by the time we returned."

It was merely a minor disappointment for us that we could not reach his orchard-garden, but for Idelfonso, lack of access to his crops following a tropical storm or hurricane was much more. Weed seeds wash in and germinate. Roots rot. Insects hatch, and their foraging on the crop plants take its toll in innumerable ways, including the spread of insect-vectored viruses and other diseases. It was late in the season and many of his crops were already harvested, but Idelfonso's work was not completely done out there.

The seemingly tranquil, laid-back village of Chacsinkin was beset with anxieties, just as any farm town in the world might be in this present day and age. The market for habaneros from Yucatán was on the rise as global demand for fiery hot foods grew exponentially. That meant that habaneros were not merely a Mayan subsistence crop for local use in "dog's-nose" salsas and such, but a cash cow as well.

And yet timing needed to be right on the money to take full advantage of such opportunities. Idelfonso had to plant on time, harvest the bulk of his crop when going prices were peaking, and beat his competitors to a buyer-broker willing to drive all the way to Chacsinkin to take his harvest and put cash in his hands. Hurricanes and tropical storms threw a bunch of wild cards on the table, reducing the chances that everything would run just like clockwork.

Idelfonso's broad face broke out into a smile now and then, but most of the time he was intensely serious as he talked about his village's agricultural economy, for he insisted that we gain a sense of all the variables with which he and his neighbors needed to contend. As the sun began to fall behind the mango, papaya, guamúchil, and ceiba tree canopies on the horizon, he realized that we still needed to drive all the way back to Mérida and that it would be dark before we arrived in the city. He suggested to Jorge that we stop on our way back through Muna to get some "carry-out" food to tide us over until we reached the city. Jorge

# The Pungent Principle

You've probably heard of capsaicin before: It's the main culprit among an entire class of molecules that are the reason for the pain and pleasure in chile peppers, and probably the sole reason why humans began to domesticate chile peppers in the first place, some seven thousand years ago. There are nine different capsaicinoids that trigger a physiological response. The most important of these nine is capsaicin, which makes up about 70 percent of all capsaicinoids found in your average chile pepper. Capsaicinoids are hydrophobic molecules, meaning they don't like water and will not dissolve in pure water. Which should put to rest the common perception that to quench your pepper-scorched mouth you should drink cold water. On the contrary, you need something with some oil or fat to wash it away—try milk, yogurt, or ice cream.

Capsaicin triggers a physiological response in all mammals. In humans, the body reacts to capsaicin as it reacts to elevated temperatures—in fact, areas of the body in direct contact with it experience a burning sensation. In small doses, capsaicin increases mucus secretion in the lungs and nose and causes a release of endorphins, creating an effect similar to the runner's high, which can be an addictive feeling—hence the comparisons to substance dependency with chileheads, who just have to have a little heat in everything they eat.

Evolutionarily speaking, capsaicin is a plant defense mechanism that evolved over time. What makes this a great tool is that birds do not have the same ability to "taste" this heat, and seeds pass right through their gut. This allows the birds to consume chile fruits and later disperse the seeds through their excrement, while at the same time deterring rodents and other mammals that might damage or destroy the seeds while consuming them or the fruits. Recently, it has also been noted that wild populations of a pepper with a genetic mutation that makes them non-pungent are more likely to experience fungal infections in the seeds, effectively killing them. Whether fungi or mammals, capsaicin will burn anything in defense of the seeds—something to keep in mind the next time you seek a chile fix.

Kraig

and Idelfonso both knew one of Rogelio's aunts who lived in that town and who made some of the spiciest foods around. Jorge agreed that we should try out her home cooking. We all shook hands with Idelfonso, wished him well, hopped into the Spice Ship, and hit the road once more.

Once we had arrived in Muna, we got lost along its narrow streets trying to find Rogelio's home and his aunt's out-of-the-front-porch bakery a block or so away. We had almost given up when Rogelio's daughter spotted Jorge, flagged him down, and told us that Rogelio and Guadalupe Isabel had just come back from the farm and were on their way over to Rogelio's aunt's place as well. She gave us directions detailed enough to get us within sight of Rogelio's smiling face.

He was out in the street, clowning around, pretending to flag us down. He shook hands with us once again.

"You're in luck, my aunt has just made some *mucpil pollo,* a special dish that most people only make for the Day of the Dead. But hers is *so* good that after the *Dia de los Muertos,* the neighbors beg her to keep making it for several weeks more."

It was one of the traditional Mayan foods that most interested Kurt, since it used minced habaneros in a broth to infuse a tamale-like cake with their flavors and piquancy, rather than making the peppers into a salsa to put on top of the dish. Kraig couldn't wait and grabbed his fork as Rogelio's aunt brought out the first *pib* cake, breaking into it before Gary had a chance to take a photo. Kraig was relieved as Rogelio's aunt brought out another *pib* cake.

"What are you guys going to eat?" Kraig joked as he started to blow on a forkful of the oven-hot *pib*.

It had been wrapped in banana leaves, adorned with a chicken bone on top, baked in the ground in a traditional Mayan oven (*pib*), and resurfaced just minutes before our arrival. When we opened up the banana leaves and dipped our spoons into this baked corn pie, our mouths watered and our tongues burned. The habaneros' heat had spread to every morsel of cornmeal, meat, and onion in the entire savory cake. It offered us a deliciously slow burn just below our thresholds of pain.

In other words, eating the *pib* was intensely pleasurable, and deeply memorable.

And perhaps that's how peppers should be. They should remind us that the best food is more than mere calories that nourish our bodies; it also sparks our imaginations and stimulates and challenges us to stretch our tolerances beyond what we could have ever previously imagined.

# Ceviche *(Escabeche)*

A handy rule of thumb to judge any Mexican, Caribbean, or Central or South American restaurant is to check out their ceviche (in Castilian Spanish, *escabeche*). If they don't make a good ceviche, you should consider taking your business elsewhere. It is such a staple in the cuisines of any of these cultures—the ones with seashores at any rate—that if they cannot make ceviche well, their abilities with anything else should be called into question. Especially since it is so simple to make.

Many folks are put off by the fact that the seafood in ceviche never sees any heat. Don't be. Although it is never heated, the fish is nonetheless fully cooked. Instead of using heat, the proteins are broken down by citric acid, through a process called denaturation, which "cooks" the fish or shellfish, tenderizing it and adding flavor at the same time.

Ceviche is one of those dishes that has as many varieties as it has cooks, cuisines, and cultures. Not only is it popular throughout the southern half of this hemisphere, it is beloved across the northern Mediterranean, Southeast Asia, and Polynesia. Notably, that's everywhere the Spanish sailed in their heyday. It may be debated among food historians just where the dish originated, but there is little doubt that it was the Spanish who, while they did not create it first, certainly loved it enough to spread it around the world.

While quick to prepare, it does need to be made a little in advance, since the effect that the citric acid has on the seafood can take anywhere from twenty minutes to two hours, depending on which fish or shellfish you choose and how it is cut. Nearly any type of seafood will suffice, but the most popular ceviches are made with flaky whitefish, shrimp, and/or scallops. The recipe below is for a simple one, but once you understand the technique, the limits are only those of imagination.

1 pound scallops

1 shallot, julienned

½ cup julienned roasted red bell peppers

2 tablespoons chopped fresh cilantro

1 lemon, juiced

1 orange, juiced

1 lime, juiced

1 orange, supremed (remove the segments from between the piths, so they look like the canned mandarin type)

To clean the scallops, rinse them thoroughly in cold water, drain, then inspect each one for a small, tough, extra piece of flesh clinging to the side of the cylindrical form of the scallop. This is called the foot and should be removed, as it is tough and chewy. Then simply pat each scallop dry on a paper towel and slice across the grain into little "coins."

Mix the scallops with the rest of the ingredients and let sit, refrigerated, for at least an hour (or to taste), stirring often to coat the scallops with citrus juice. Serve as a salad or appetizer, or even as a garnish for grilled fish. *Serves 4-6.*

## *Pollo Pibil*

The perfect use for *recado rojo* and *xnipek* (see the recipes that follow) is this Yucatecan classic. It is a simpler relative of an old Mayan recipe called *mucbil pollo*, which has found its way into some American homes as a tamale pie. *Pibil* does not use masa–the dough part of the tamale–but like *mucbil* it is wrapped in banana leaves, both for flavor and to help it retain moisture. It is ubiquitous throughout the Yucatán.

In the aforementioned book *Foods of the Maya*, Nancy Gerlach recommends the hard-to-find *x'catic* or güero chiles, but a few other varieties may suffice, according to your heat preferences. The recipe below calls for habaneros purely for impact, but since you'll want to serve this with your new batch of *xnipek*, you may choose to tone it down a little.

The banana leaves may seem hard to come by, but they are easily available in nearly any Asian market, and now in many bodegas. They come frozen and will last in your freezer almost indefinitely, so don't fret about the packages that have too many. They're cheap, and they can also be used as a tasty substitute for the corn husks around tamales, or to wrap around fish for the grill. If you're adventurous, you might even use them for that *mucbil pollo*. The recipe also calls for a Mexican herb called epazote. It's hard to find it fresh sometimes, but every bodega has it in its dried form, which will suffice here.

*Pibil* is traditionally cooked over open coals, but your home oven will work just fine. For the deepest flavor, start a day ahead so your chicken has time to marinate. Serve with the traditional rice and black beans.

**6 boneless, skinless chicken breasts**
**Salt to taste**
**½ cup *recado rojo***

1 cup bitter orange juice (or see the substitute on page 99)

2 banana leaves

2 tablespoons olive oil

2 tablespoons butter

1 yellow onion, julienned

2 habanero chiles, stemmed, seeded, and chopped (or to taste)

2 banana chiles, or 1 sweet bell pepper, julienned

2 cloves garlic, sliced paper-thin

2 tablespoons dried, rubbed epazote

## A Day Before Service

Using a sharp paring knife, score the skin side of the chicken four to six times, diagonally across the grain, to allow the marinade to penetrate. Season lightly with salt and place the breasts in a shallow baking dish. Mix the *recado* and bitter orange juice and pour over the chicken. Turn each breast once to thoroughly coat with the marinade, then cover and refrigerate overnight.

## Ninety Minutes Before Service

Preheat your oven to 350°F. Line a second baking dish (or wash and reuse the first) with the banana leaves, cut to allow enough extra to make flaps that will fold over the top to cover. Place the chicken, scored side up, in the leaves and add the remaining marinade.

In a large sauté pan, heat the olive oil and butter over a medium-high flame, then add the onion, chiles, garlic, and epazote and sauté until the vegetables are tender. Add just a dash of salt, then pour the mixture over the chicken. Wrap the excess banana leaves over the top of the chicken, and bake for 45 minutes. Remove from the oven and allow to rest for 15 minutes, then serve.

If you have leftovers, this dish makes a fantastic chicken salad. Simply chop it all up and toss with a little mayo and lime juice. *Serves 6.*

## *Recado Rojo*

Alongside the habanero, the other distinctive flavor of the Yucatán is *recado*, a tradition that dates back to well before the arrival of the conquistadores. Made in several colors, it is a flavoring paste comprising many different herbs and spices. The distinctive red color of the *recado rojo* is derived from the use of annatto, the natural red food coloring from the achiote tree that carries with it its own sweet peppery notes.

In the enormous central market of downtown Mérida, you can see many different vendors making the various pastes and piling them high on their counters to be sold by the kilo to chefs and traditional home cooks alike. It's so simple to make, however, that it's a wonder everyone in the region doesn't make their own, though of course many do.

Each of the different colors has traditional uses. The green is for *bistec*, or beef steak; the black and sometimes gritty one is for turkey. *Recado rojo* is surely the most popular, and it is the key to chicken *pibil*, a classic Yucatecan pork dish cooked in banana leaves (see page 94).

This version is a derivation. Kurt began with the recipe in Nancy and Jeffrey Gerlach's excellent *Foods of the Maya: A Taste of the Yucatán* (University of New Mexico Press, 1994) and then just started tweaking, as is his wont. The whole key is a balance of flavors, which is extremely subjective, so start with this recipe and see where it takes you. Most people will use a spice grinder, which is no more than a retasked coffee grinder, but, to be authentic, use a mortar and pestle. One caveat, though: Whole annatto seeds are extremely hard to grind, so look for the powdered form in almost any neighborhood bodega.

**8 whole black peppercorns**
**1-inch cinnamon stick**

5 whole cloves

2 allspice berries

1 teaspoon toasted cumin seeds

½ teaspoon salt

¼ cup ground annatto seeds

2 tablespoons dried Mexican oregano (it makes a difference that you use the
  Mexican variety)

4 cloves garlic, peeled

3 tablespoons sour orange juice or cider vinegar

If you are using a spice grinder, grind the pepper, cinnamon, cloves, allspice, and toasted cumin seeds together to a fine powder. Then transfer to a blender, add the remaining ingredients, and pulverize into a smooth paste. Add a little water if it helps to get a better consistency.

It's a little different if you use a mortar and pestle. Begin by crushing the pepper and cinnamon, then add the cloves and continue to grind. Add the allspice and the cumin and grind to a coarse powder. Toss in the annatto and oregano, mix, then add the salt and garlic and begin to pulverize into a paste, adding the juice or vinegar a little at a time, and a little water to help with the consistency. Remember what Play-Doh felt like when you were a kid? That's the consistency you're looking for.

The *recado* will last, sealed tightly in the refrigerator, for weeks. *Yields about ½ cup.*

# Genuine *Xnipek*

One of the most delightful food discoveries for us in Mérida was *xnipek* (pronounced SHNEE-peck). The name comes from the Mayan language and means "dog's nose." Unappetizing as that might sound at first, rest assured there is no dog in the recipe. It's simply a reference to this salsa's heat level. Hot chiles can cause the nose to run, thus the metaphor.

There's more to *xnipek* than just heat, though. It not only uses the Yucatecan powerhouse chile—the habanero—but also includes the Arabic fruit known as *naranja agria*, or bitter orange, which is also the secret to great Yucatecan *escabeche*. It's hard to find fresh in the States, so there's a brief recipe for a reasonable facsimile following our rendition of this fiery relish.

We found many versions of *xnipek* in our travels around the Yucatán. All had the habanero and bitter orange, but beyond that they varied widely. This is why we prefer the term *genuine* to *authentic*—it allows for many interpretations while still remaining true to tradition.

*Xnipek* is one of the salsas collectively referred to as *pico de gallo*, or "beak of the chicken," a reference either to the size of the chopped ingredients or to chicken feed. It's made of many ingredients chopped together to form more of a relish than a sauce (or salsa). Our favorite renditions include the unique addition of fresh cabbage, which adds another layer of flavor and crunch.

½ cup chopped or shredded green cabbage
2 fresh habanero chiles, seeded and minced (you could substitute any chile, but you'd lose the right to call it "genuine")
2 medium-ripe tomatoes, cored and diced
1 red onion, peeled and diced

½ cup fresh-squeezed bitter orange juice (or use the facsimile, below, but stick with fresh juices)
3–4 tablespoons chopped fresh cilantro

Soak the cabbage in ice water for an hour or so to make it crispy. Drain and dry thoroughly using a salad spinner or paper towels.

Toss the cabbage together with the habaneros, tomatoes, onion, and bitter orange juice. Let stand at room temperature for a couple of hours, or in the refrigerator overnight, then add the fresh chopped cilantro right before service. *Yields around 2 cups.*

### Makeshift Bitter Orange Juice

Combine in a 2:1:1 ratio fresh-squeezed grapefruit juice, orange juice, and lime juice. Let stand for an hour. It will keep in the refrigerator, covered, for up to 1 day.

# CHAPTER FOUR

# Tabascos: A Cure for That Sinking Feeling in Cajun Country

**AS THE SPICE SHIP** began to circle over New Orleans on November 17, 2009, we wondered whether we would be seeing the same residues of floods from Hurricane Ida in Louisiana as we had just seen in the Yucatán a week earlier. While we were still in Mexico on November 9, Hurricane Ida had been downgraded to a tropical storm. From what we could pick up from news channels, she was about to make landfall near Mobile Bay, east of New Orleans.

The tempest had dropped less than a couple of inches of rain on New Orleans, which was spared this time. But Ida gained steam again as she moved northward, dumping four to five inches of rain on Appalachia, and raising the water level in Kerr Lake, North Carolina, to ten feet above its normal level. From there, she danced her way up toward New England, knocking out power in more than 150,000 homes, killing six people, and flooding beach towns along the shores of New York and New Jersey.

Although Louisiana was spared a direct hit from the tropical storm, as we came from the southwest toward New Orleans, the roads around Bayou Bois Piquant and Lake Cataouatche all looked flooded. Water stood in all the highway medians and was covering every other depression as far as we could see around Louis Armstrong International Airport.

After we had refueled and grabbed some provisions, we headed toward Lafayette around midday. As we drove along, Kraig pointed out tilted telephone poles along the roadsides and canals past Lake Pontchartrain and Lake Maurepas. We saw similar poles off-kilter just west of Baton Rouge, all the way along the edges of Des Ourses Swamp.

Cajun Country was up to its neck in murky water just about everywhere we looked. But our first impressions of the cause of all this high water proved wrong. Yes, every body of water we passed was indeed swollen, but Ida had not been the cause. In fact, what we were seeing in Cajun Country along the Gulf Coast was close to the norm, if that Acadian stretch of Louisiana has a norm anymore.

As we later found out, a long, convoluted chain of events is causing the rising waters in the Mississippi Delta. Human activities have interrupted the cyclical rejuvenation of the delta lands, from the construction of dikes and dams on the Mississippi River itself to the creation of other canals, channels, and diversions, which are the main drivers causing the subsidence of the delta and its islands in the bayous. As these lands disappear, there is a subsequent loss of coastal wetlands, and open water replaces marshy vegetation.

One of the most infamous of these canals was the Mississippi River Gulf Outlet canal—known as MRGO, often pronounced as *Mr. Go*. Mr. Go is a seventy-six-mile-long canal created by the Army Corps of Engineers, which decreased the length of the shipping route from the Gulf of Mexico to the inner harbor of New Orleans by fifty miles. The construction of Mr. Go resulted in the immediate loss of more than eight thousand acres of marshes and wetlands, and since its construction an untold number of acres due to the saltwater intrusion and increased erosion. Once a canal only sixty feet wide, there are sections that today measure over three hundred feet across. During Hurricane Katrina, the Gulf opening of Mr. Go acted like a funnel, channeling the storm surge straight into the canals of inner New Orleans, offering a straight shot into the heart of the city. It is thought that the increased strain on the levees brought on by Mr. Go's "funnel" effect greatly contributed to the failure of the levees. After Hurricane Katrina, the US Army Corps of Engineers finally decided to close Mr. Go.

While Mr. Go is probably the largest example, it is not the only canal in the wetlands. After decades of aggressive hydrological engineering upstream, the Mississippi Delta has been starved of sediments that would have normally been deposited through the periodic flooding of the region. The barrier islands have been so denuded of vegetation that they are simply eroding away, for there has been almost no replenishment of their soils.

This sort of environmental degradation, of course, is not unique to the delta of the Mississippi. In northern California, the islands in the delta of the Sacramento River have subsided to the point that their "summits" sit below the water level of the river. In fact, they are now separated from the waters only by dikes and levees. And deltas on nearly every major river with dams upstream now face a similar fate.

The barely perceptible rise of ocean levels is just as worrisome over the long haul, as warmer global air temperatures and the melting of the planet's polar ice caps fuel it. It has yet to have a significant effect on the Mississippi River Delta compared with the perverse ecological legacy of the oil and natural gas companies working in the Gulf: the dredging of channels and clearing of rights-of-way for pipelines and service roads. These linear excavations run inland from the ocean-front and further disrupt the delicate balance of nature along the Gulf Coast, for they facilitate saltwater intrusion into the deeper parts of basins and bayous. As a result of this combination of natural and human-made factors, some 1.2 million acres of the delta—an area the size of Delaware—was lost in the span of a normal human lifetime, in the years between 1930 and 2000.

These are the cold, hard facts, yet they don't capture the devastation of bayou life as much as images do. Picture fishing camps—some which your family might have frequented for a century or more—slowly sinking into the ever-widening waterways, taking your chinaberry and

◀ *Chiles de sarta*, pickled chiltepin, and other local products for sale on the side of the highway, near Magdalena de Kino, Sonora. (Kurt Friese)

▼ Strings of *chiles de sarta*, near Magdalena de Kino, Sonora. (Kurt Friese)

▲ The authors after lunch in the dining room of Jesús and Casimiro Sanchez in San Ignacio, Sonora. (Kim McWane Friese)

▶ A Yaqui vendor shows us the green chiltepin he is sorting, Cocorit, Sonora. (Gary Nabhan)

▲ Casimiro Sanchez in his family's orchard, San Ignacio, Sonora. (Kraig Kraft)

◀ These Sonoran chiles from the garden grow easily in the fields and are replacing the wild chiltepin on kitchen tables. (Kurt Friese)

▲ Native American spiritual leader Bobby Billie leading a prayer before our event in St. Augustine. (Kurt Friese)

▲ Datil peppers. (Kurt Friese)

▲ Kurt and Kraig get up close with some greenhouse datil peppers. (Gary Nabhan)

▲ Johnny Barnes with smoked mullet, pulled from the intercoastal waterway of St. Augustine, Florida. (Kurt Friese)

▲ Mayan habaneros in a market in Ticul, Yucatán. (Kraig Kraft)

▲ Guadalupe Isabel Vargas Ku in her habanero patch, Muna, Yucatán. (Kraig Kraft)

▲ Just picked habaneros, Yucatán, Mexico. (Kraig Kraft)

▲ Handfuls of habaneros, Ticul, Yucatán.
(Gary Nabhan)

▶ Habanero vendor in a Mayan market in
Ticul, Yucatán. (Gary Nabhan)

▲ A piping hot *moc pib pollo*—a tamale pie filled with habanero laced chicken, in Muna, Yucatán. (Gary Nabhan)

▲ Tabasco peppers in the field at Avery Island, Louisiana. (Kraig Kraft)

▲ Harold Osborn and Gary examine ripening tabasco peppers on Avery Island, Louisiana. (Kraig Kraft)

▲ The variegated fruits of the fish pepper in George Washington's Birthplace, Virginia. (Kraig Kraft)

lemon trees, your mirliton vines and pepper bushes with them. Houma Indians, Cajuns, Creole blacks, and others who have long depended on the coastal wetlands as their nursery grounds for shrimp, redfish, flounder, and oysters now wonder where, or if, their seafood stocks will be replenished. They look out across a vast expanse of water and remember where their family's fish camps once were, just like a soldier wounded in action feels his "phantom limb" long after it is amputated.

To put it another way, Cajun Country was no longer on solid ground, terra firma. It looked and smelled more like a shellfish gumbo, with a few specks of land floating in a thick, dark broth.

As we mulled over these issues, we headed west to Lafayette to visit with some chefs, chile producers, food historians, and musicians, including the members of the aptly named Lost Bayou Ramblers. We were hoping to get their particular perspectives on the unique local flavors and the changes they have experienced in harvesting food from their increasingly waterlogged landscape From there, we would head south to New Iberia and Avery Island—the home of McIlhenny Company, maker of Tabasco® hot sauce—for that is the epicenter of both pepper history and hot sauce production in Louisiana.

We had come to Acadiana to ponder in particular the relationship between tabasco peppers and Cajun culture, and their lore about changes along the Gulf Coast. Although our visit predated the *Deepwater Horizon* oil spill, we wanted to know how the Cajun farmers and fishers who remained in their homeland were coping with hurricanes, human out-migration, floods, viruses, and a host of other changes.

The tabasco pepper—used in the most famous hot sauce made in America—began its meteoric rise to immortality right here in the heart of Cajun Country. Today you can find that sauce in more than 165 countries and territories worldwide. Our GIs are deployed with tiny bottles in their MREs (meals ready to eat). In some of those countries, Tabasco sauce is not merely an American icon, it is ever-present on the kitchen table.

Once the sole site for commercial production of tabasco peppers, Avery Island now reserves its limited arable lands for a small population of pepper plants that produce all the seeds used in the global production of Tabasco sauces. More than forty years ago, some very smart folks at McIlhenny Company decided that, to protect their supply from economic and environmental uncertainties, the production of tabasco peppers needed to be spread beyond Cajun Country, to several nations in both Central and South America.

To a large measure, this dispersal of tabasco pepper production means that McIlhenny no longer keeps all its chiles in one basket. In many ways, the diversified strategies of McIlhenny Company are a model for coping with uncertainty—they offer resilience in the face of increasingly unpredictable ecological and cultural conditions.

The company's portfolio of adaptive strategies seemed to us the harbinger of what was to come, not just for tabasco peppers, but for many place-based crops, and their products and producers. If we could fathom how tabasco peppers had stayed tethered to Cajun Country while at the same time adapting to all kinds of new challenges, conditions, and countries, we felt we might better understand what might happen to other heritage foods and their *terroirs* over the next half century.

But for the moment, we were following the Louisiana Culinary Trail out of its Creole hub of New Orleans into the heart of Acadiana, where Cajun cuisine and Tabasco sauce first caught fire. As Kurt drove us across the Mississippi at Baton Rouge, Gary picked up The Gator on the radio—KROF 960 AM—and the *lingua franca* of the airwaves shifted from English to Cajun French. We caught a few bars of Louis Michot of the Lost Bayou Ramblers singing "La Bouteille a Ruiné Ma Vie," an old drinking song from Vermilion Bay, just a hot breath away from Avery Island's pepper patches. The next song we heard was "Hot Chili Mama," sung by Michael Doucet of the band BeauSoleil. Those songs made Kraig thirsty and hungry enough to pull out his stash of road food and drink. He passed around a small sample of Zapp's Spicy Creole Tomato Tabasco Potato Chips, another of Zapp's Mardi Gras Cajun Crawtators, and still another of Zapp's Spicy Creole Tomato. When we grew tired of chips, he shared some fresh boudin sausage, a

Cajun Country staple that is a riff on classic French charcuterie, which he had picked up at a truck stop outside Baton Rouge.

As our mouths sung with the familiar Tabasco burn, we tried to absorb all the imagery that the Spice Ship was passing, trying to make sense of this peculiar place. There is nothing like immersing yourself in the local flavors and local sounds to make a person feel like he has arrived at someplace truly different. And Acadiana, Louisiana, is a place like no other.

That night, after meeting up with several friends in Lafayette, we drove twenty miles out along levees and through cane fields toward Henderson, on the edge of the Atchafalaya Basin. We had set our sights on Robin's Restaurant, pronounced *row-baan's* by local folk, for a true Cajun meal. Within seconds of entering the door, we were greeted by chef Lionel Robin, who is as much a duck hunter, bird dog breeder, storyteller, and raconteur as he is a renowned Cajun chef. Lionel has not only cooked *with* Tabasco sauce most of his life; for decades, he has known and cooked *for* Paul McIlhenny, the seasoned president and CEO of McIlhenny Company. Their friendship harks back to the days when they served together in the Marine Reserves. Among Chef Lionel's many culinary achievements are some fifty kinds of gumbo—no two of them alike—and his recipe for Tabasco ice cream, a delicacy that is so hot that you have to eat more of it just to cool yourself off.

Lionel did not merely give us a perfunctory greeting, only to disappear back into the kitchen for the rest of the evening; his curiosity about our mission had been piqued, so he sat down with us and stayed for the long haul.

By *long haul* at Robin's, what we mean is that, over the next three hours, half a dozen of us engaged in the leisurely sampling of five distinctive gumbos, frog legs étoufée, crab étoufée, some boulettes, a smoky and savory crab plate, and a couple of bottles of wine. When we began to wind down on the more savory dishes, Lionel directed us toward the sweets: a delicate fig ice cream, and then his incendiary Tabasco ice cream as a final send-off. (Lionel spikes a gallon of house-made vanilla ice cream base with a two-ounce bottle of the original Tabasco hot sauce.)

Today McIlhenny Company markets five distinct hot sauces, but the one based on salt, vinegar, and the fermented mash of tabasco peppers dates back to the 1860s and is called the *original* Tabasco sauce. It is one of the few commercial hot sauces made anywhere in the world with the semi-domesticated peppers of *Capsicum frutescens*. Of the five domesticated species of chile peppers, *C. frutescens* is the only one without varieties that have been clearly domesticated beyond the wild forms—tabasco, the Brazilian malagueta, and the African bird's eye are the only named varieties, and one can argue that they are only semi-domesticated. None of these named cultivars is produced on any sizable scale. Even though its commercial production could still be called artisanal, Tabasco is arguably the most widely recognized pepper sauce in the world, and the best-selling bottled substance of any kind for fanning the flames of fiery food and saucy drink.

Oddly enough, its migrations from Mexico to Louisiana are so complex and convoluted that Louisiana historian Shane K. Bernard has collected four distinctively different oral histories of how and when this Latin American pepper arrived in Louisiana around the time of the Civil War—three of the four from McIlhenny family members themselves. Perhaps what matters more than the historical minutiae is that ever since 1868, when Edmund McIlhenny first wrote out a particular recipe for combining the mash of tabasco peppers with salt and vinegar into a savory sauce, that recipe has remained constantly in use, unaltered. Although the crop plants themselves are grown in other places now, the ripe peppers are ground, mixed with salt, and shipped back to Avery Island, where all the Tabasco sauce consumed in the world is still produced, with Cajun hands involved.

According to one version of family tradition, just after the Civil War a Confederate soldier named Gleason returned from Tabasco, Mexico, to New Orleans, where he reputedly gave Edmund McIlhenny a few dried, seed-laden pods of a tabasco pepper. This one was clearly a distinctive member of the genus *Capsicum,* of red pepper fame.

Gardeners in Louisiana may have grown several peppers from eastern Mexico for some time. But it wasn't until 1888 that Edmund's *tabasco pepper* became a common name for this heirloom variety in the newly described species *Capsicum frutescens,* for which botanists used one of his plants as the "type specimen." A century and a half later, it remains the only variety of that pepper species grown on any scale in the United States.

Over most of that time, tabasco peppers have been commercially grown only within spitting distance of Vermilion Bay, a brackish body of water fed by bayous that opens onto the Gulf of Mexico. Year after year, the sowing of their heirloom seeds has been rotated through some sixty acres of arable land amid the twenty-two hundred acres of an arching salt dome historically known as Petite Anse. The island sanctuary of Petite Anse sits not far from the main channel of Vermilion Bay, and its harbors on the Gulf side have been used by hunters, fishermen, and salt miners for hundreds of years. But not too many years after Petite Anse was bought lock, stock, and barrel by the Avery family, its post office was designated as Avery's Island, and soon the entire salt dome came to be known as Avery Island.

It is a world unto itself, housing many of the Avery and McIlhenny family descendants as well as hot sauce pickers and processors, salt miners, oil drillers, thousands of tropical plants, and hundreds of thousands of migratory birds.

Oddly enough, Avery Island contains some of the highest and safest land along the entire Gulf Coast, for the salt dome topography pushes the promontories of Petite Anse as high as 163 feet above sea level. Compared with most of the barrier islands and shorelines of the Gulf Coast, the uplands of Avery Island are akin to a Cajun Mount Ararat, the veritable mountain sanctuary where Noah supposedly landed the Ark. That's because several times within recent human memory, nearly all the fields and yards for miles around have been underwater, either because of catastrophic events like the Great Flood of 1927 and Hurricane Rita, or because of saltwater intrusion and the insidious expansion of bays and bayous as much of the Mississippi Delta sinks into the Gulf. As Cajun shrimper Papoose Ledet told travel writer Mike Tidwell for Tidwell's heartbreakingly beautiful eulogy, *Bayou Farewell:*

> We're *sinking*. Sinking. And not just a little. Dey say every twenty minutes or so, a football field of land turns into water in Louisiana . . . Dey got satellite photos from outer space showing how much land we're losing every year. It'll make your hair stand up to see it.

When we met with Louis Michot, a Cajun fiddler whose family has lived around Broussard, Louisiana, since 1765, we quickly gained a sense of why he calls his band the Lost Bayou Ramblers. "Have I seen the water levels change in the bayous since I was a kid? Well sure, not so much up where I'm living near Lafayette, but you can definitely see it down where some of our family has always gone to fish . . . like Bayou LaFourche, where the stretches of open water have surely gotten bigger. You go down to an old Cajun place, say like Golden Meadow, and just about all of it is underwater anymore."

As we drove around Cajun Country over several days, it was hard to shake a rather spooky feeling: Almost every *land*scape looked like a Black Lagoon, with something ominous hidden right below its surface. Acadiana was like a sponge—it was so saturated with moisture that it would be hard to find many spots where tabasco peppers might keep their feet dry enough to be free of fungi and molds.

The ubiquity of rising water begged the question: How long can tabasco peppers remain in Acadiana without picking up their roots and moving to higher ground, just as many Cajuns have done? In the four years following in the wake of Hurricanes Katrina and Rita, one out of every ten Louisiana residents moved out of state, but in the southern parishes of Cajun Country, that ratio had been closer to three to five in ten. This out-migration has further crippled the capacity of the remnant workforce in rural areas, which had already been in decline. In the 1960s, pepper pickers had hand-harvested thousands of acres of tabasco, cayenne, and sweet bell peppers in Louisiana, but pepper agriculture in Acadiana today is but a shadow of its former self. Not even a quarter of the pepper fields harvested during Louisiana's agricultural heyday are even planted anymore.

And so one pair of questions and answers begs another: Have environmental changes triggered by shifting weather patterns—in the form of rising sea levels and more frequent storms—been directly responsible for the decline of pepper patches and the out-migration of Cajuns from Louisiana? Not really, as of yet. Instead, the cause of Louisiana's historic losses of twenty-five square miles of marshlands and low-lying fields per year still has more to do with the subsidence of lands that have been chronically starved of sediments over the last century than it does with shifting global climate.

Nevertheless, the climate-driven changes that have been smaller players on the Gulf Coast—from increasingly violent hurricanes to rising global sea levels—are projected to become more and more prominent influences in the overall mix. While scientists must be careful not to read *climate, climate, climate* into every tragic scene they see, they would be burying their heads in the sand if they ignored it as one of several interlocking factors that are disrupting farming and fisheries on the Gulf Coast.

We headed down the road from Lafayette to New Iberia, the former capital (or Mother Church, depending on one's devotion) in all of Acadiana for chile peppers. In the 1950s and '60s, it was the center of all pepper production in the state, with a new hot sauce factory built every couple of years. New Iberia is the home to Trappey's Hot Sauce, and it also gave birth to Louisiana Hot Sauce, Red Devil Hot Sauce, and Chef-Magic Hot Sauce. Not to mention the fact that McIlhenny and its Tabasco sauce production facilities are just nine more miles out of town to the southwest.

Driving into New Iberia from the north, however, we initially saw few clues to this rich, flavorful past. No pepper fields were visible from the roads, only the occasional sugarcane plot; there were no giant hot sauce superstores, no plaques or historical markers. New Iberia seemed

# Tabasco

### *(Capsicum frutescens)*

Of the five species of chile pepper that humans have domesticated, this is the one that comes with an asterisk. There is a *small* problem: By definition, the species is not quite fully domesticated. Sure, the tabasco pepper belongs to this species, and so do the malagueta of Brazil and the African bird's eye pepper; but the species is feral–these varieties and their ilk are found in home gardens, backyards, fence lines, and the like. The lone exception is the tabasco pepper, which is grown solely for the purposes of making Tabasco hot sauce. The hallmarks of domestication in chile peppers are agreed to be the following characteristics: pendant, or hanging, fruit (as opposed to erect and upright fruit), larger fruit size, and ripe fruit staying on the plant rather than falling (lack of an "abscission layer" in technical terms), among others. Looking at the plant, it is a compact and dense bush, with conical two-inch fruits that point up. When the fruit ripens from green to fingernail-polish red, just a small touch or tap knocks it off the plant–an old evolutionary dispersal mechanism, allowing birds to harvest the fruit and disperse the seeds. Humans have bred these traits out of other domesticated chile species, but they persist in *C. frutescens,* which definitely owes a debt of gratitude to the folks who make Tabasco sauce at McIlhenny Company, without whom we might not even cultivate this species at all. In fact, it is difficult to separate the species and the handful of varieties from Tabasco, the hot sauce. Tabasco sauce represents 99 percent of the commercial endeavors and commercialization of this species.

When we talk about Tabasco sauce, there are a number of superlatives that come up–*old, American, genuine*–and one that is probably fitting in many ways: *first.* As in a first experience or exposure to spicy food, hot sauce, or chile peppers. There is a special spot in our

to be one of the sleepier towns of the Gulf Coast, as if it had shrunk back a bit from its heyday, with some abandoned storefronts hinting at its earlier, globally recognized glories.

As we ate a late breakfast in Victor's Cafeteria in New Iberia—the favorite haunt of Cajun detective David Robicheaux in James Lee Burke's novels—we could hear, at every other table, retirees and old-timers inevitably talking about the weather. Four to six people sat talking around each of the simple wooden tables that were cluttered with plates of grits, fried eggs, biscuits and gravy, and little bottles of Tabasco and Louisiana Hot sauces. These were the same people whom Burke memory banks for firsts–we remember these moments with a vividness that is lacking in other memories. First kiss, first car, first pet, baby's first words, first time traveling away from home. But if you are wired for chile peppers and spicy foods, you remember your first fiery bites. And for the majority of Americans who don't live in New Mexico or near the Mexican border, or call their grandmother *abuela*, their first encounter with spicy food is usually a tussle with Tabasco. It was for me.

I was maybe seven years old, sitting down to a Saturday breakfast of over-easy fried eggs and some toast, and I added my usual dollop of ketchup. See, I had this thing–I loved mixing the bright yellow yolk with the dark red ketchup like I was mixing inks on a paint palette. I'd take the pieces of toast, break them into small chunks, soak up the mixture, and draw my masterpiece on my plate, finally consuming my toast-brush. Once the toast supply was dwindling, I'd use it as an eraser to clean up my ephemeral drawing, timing the last of the toast with clearing the last of the orange designs–my own edible Etch A Sketch. The Tabasco bottle lived next to the ketchup in the cupboard, and one day, out of curiosity– either because of its red color (*maybe it will make lighter shades of orange?*) or because the ketchup was running low–I sprayed some on my eggs. I was a bit disappointed at how thin the sauce came out, but, determined to get the best orange hue for my drawings, I broke the yolks with my fork and mixed it as well as I could. And while I would like to say that this was a moment of pure transcendence and enlightenment, it didn't quite happen that way. In fact, it took me a while before I put it back on my eggs. Now I can't eat eggs without hot sauce or chile peppers, but when I use Tabasco, the inimitable smell brings me right back to that morning as a seven-year-old at the breakfast table.

Kraig

described, folks who "could not eat anything without cayenne or black pepper gumbo filé in it."

They wove any changes in the weather into everything else they said. "Is de hurricane season really over?" "Do dey still have de sump-pump a-goin dat dey put on over at de pit right when Ida came through dere?" "What dat dey left in de garden since de storm come past?"

Two of Louisiana's recent state climatologists, Barry Keim and Robert Mueller, have struggled to figure out just what part changing weather has played in the loss of pepper fields, mudbug patches (crawfish holes), and Cajun communities from the southernmost reaches of Acadiana.

> In several locations along the Gulf Coast, land is disap-
> pearing. Land gives way to sea for many reasons . . .
> The problem is most severe . . . where coastal wetlands
> have been starved of sediment since the levee system
> was erected along the Mississippi River. The river is
> no longer allowed to flood naturally across the region
> and leave behind an annual layer of sediment [that
> builds coastal wetlands] . . . This is noteworthy because
> wetlands serve as a buffer to hurricanes by absorbing
> much of the wave energy and surge.

In light of the recent destruction wrought by Hurricanes Katrina
and Rita, their latter note is particularly revealing. But they continue,
arguing that while global warming has not increased the *frequency* of
storms, it *is* one of the major factors that has affected their destructive
potential.

> Since the mid-1970s . . . the destructive potential of
> hurricanes has increased markedly due to increased
> storm lifetimes as well as increased intensities of
> storms. If global temperatures continue to rise, this
> trend should continue, and will be further exacerbated
> by increasing human developments along the coastal
> zone.

As we left New Iberia to the south, we spotted a humongous bottle of
Tabasco sauce tipped over on its side. It was up on a gigantic billboard
that simply stated, AVERY ISLAND. TURN HERE.

While we cruised along canals filled to the brim and levees topped
with mud-laden weeds, we tried to remember if there were other
times when Cajun Country had had to absorb as much water as it
had in the previous four years. Kurt recalled Randy Newman's song
"Louisiana: 1927," about the Great Flood that covered a fifty-mile-

wide, hundred-mile-long swath and caused four hundred million dollars of damage over several months of recurrent downpours. Kraig knew Aaron Neville's version, which Neville had sung on a televised Hurricane Katrina relief concert. Gary remembered the Great Flood from a hair-raising story by William Faulkner, "Old Man," published in *Wild Palms,* in which a convict ably helped rescue a young pregnant woman from a tree, but then had no idea in the world how to help her give birth while hundreds of others around them were meeting their deaths.

We later asked Shane K. Bernard, the New Iberia–based historian who works at McIlhenny's, how such disasters had affected the social fabric around New Iberia over the decades.

"People pull together," he said quietly. He rummaged through his files until he found a May 28, 1927, letter from E. A. McIlhenny to his in-law Joe Clark, of Philadelphia:

> The water situation is of course very bad. All of the farms East of Bayou Teche are now under water, and there is some danger that the farms on the West side of New Iberia South, will go under. The town of New Iberia is partly under water but not to an excessive depth, and only in the low sections have the people been obliged to move . . . I have now housed approximately 300 people, white and colored. Practically all of these are farmers, and I am pasturing their stock to the number of about 600 head, having taken all of my cattle from the prairie pasture, giving this land for the use of the farmers who are flooded. I can see no possible reason at present why your home should be occupied by refugees. If water should become several feet deeper in New Iberia this condition may change, but I don't think this is likely. If there is any material change in the situation I shall wire you.

We asked Shane about where he was when the 2005 hurricanes happened, and he grew quiet for a moment, as if it was still unsettling to think and talk about it. He started off slowly:

"I had already evacuated to Lafayette when Rita hit . . . It was the afternoon of the next day that I first came out to the island. You know, that last weekend in September, I drove out this way past New Iberia thinking that the storm was all over and that we had missed the worst of it.

"But as I was coming over to the island, I began to see things that made me worry . . . The floods were just beginning to happen. Normally, the farmworkers here would have been picking tabasco peppers around then. But it just about ruined the whole crop here. Ask Harold about it."

*Harold* was McIlhenny's vice president, Harold Osborn, who had kindly offered to host us should we ever get out to Avery Island during the growing season. We had heard that he had worked in Alaska and Africa before settling into running the crop production, research, and wetlands restoration programs for McIlhenny Company.

Before we knew it, we were out of New Iberia proper and had crossed a short toll bridge across a bayou to land on Avery Island. By midafternoon, after touring the hot sauce factory and perusing the archives, we met Harold. He was easy to talk with, worldly, and he mixed penetrating insights with unabashed humor into his own unique brand of conversational sauce. But within ten minutes of our arrival in his office, he encouraged us to jump in his vehicle so that we could see the entire island, not just the twenty acres of pepper patches hidden among the tropical vegetation there.

Harold took us by to see the pastures where E. A. McIlhenny had harbored the neighbors' livestock during the Great Flood: "Every time a flood happens, Avery Island becomes this refugee camp . . . We got hit with Ike in 2008, it wasn't just Katrina and Rita in 2005. It happens every few years, and people escape here to higher ground."

Then Harold got a theatrically strained look on his face, slowing the story down a bit to add some spice to it: "Yeah, the toughest part about

Katrina for me was that nearly all of my relatives moved in with us for three weeks!"

He laughed. "And it's not just a refugee camp for people, I gotta figure what to do with cattle, too, when our neighbors' pastures got flooded. We turned them out in one of our former fields. We had close to six hundred cattle taking sanctuary on the island for a while there. But that's how it works around here . . . if someone gets flooded, or their house or barn burns down, everyone pitches in."

Harold then drove us over to a lower-lying area that was filled with neatly maintained rows of tabasco pepper plants, still adorned with their red, yellow, and orange upright peppers. Their dark green leaves were chest-high, and the brilliantly colored peppers glimmered in the late-afternoon sunlight. We picked a few and tasted them; the heat hit us first, but then some of that characteristic Tabasco taste surfaced and stayed with us for minutes.

Below us was another experimental field of tabasco peppers, edged by a few windrows of composted pepper mash bagasse, and beyond it was a cypress swamp that Harold was helping to restore. And beyond that, the waters of Vermilion Bay shimmered out on the horizon.

We finally got around to asking Harold about the status of the fields that Shane had seen the day after Hurricane Rita. Harold was walking with a little limp when we posed the question to him. So he stopped, pointed toward the field in front of us, and then patted his leg.

"Where and how was I during Rita?" Harold's face put on a mock frown, and then he shuddered. "Well, I was around here to see what was happening, but I wasn't in too good a shape. I'd just broken my leg three weeks before. Being on crutches and Oxicodone and all that, I couldn't get around very well. When I did get out here to take a look . . ."

Harold pointed to a patch of peppers. We walked on over, into the thick of it.

". . . I was right about here, where we're standing. You couldn't go much lower than this point. The water came up to where that building is over there . . . and see those mulch piles of red mash out that way?

They'd be completely inundated over there. No, it was *more* than eight feet deep. When it surged, it was over nine, closer to ten feet over here. I mean, there were *whitecaps* on the field right out in front of us here. From here to those trees over there was *all* underwater."

We tried to imagine the shock that Harold felt when an agricultural landscape he had witnessed a thousand times over his career was suddenly transformed into a seascape. It was an eerie image, as if it were the world that Noah had witnessed on the verge of sailing off in the Ark. Gary then asked Harold what the consequences were of having one of the few tabasco pepper fields left on the island fully underwater.

"Well," Harold said with a sigh, "so we lost all the seed we would have gotten from this patch. But these are exclusively seed grow-out or research-and-development fields over here, so it's not like we had yield losses of pepper from the floods. Of course, we've got enough pepper seed stashed away in case anything happens to these plants. Anyway, we don't take out crop loss insurance, we're sort of self-insured. But keep in mind: The water surged within *just three inches* of going into our factory, the one where we make all the sauce. It did in fact come into the warehouse where we keep the mash in the oak barrels. We worked to move some of them up off the floor, but fortunately barrels can float, so we didn't really have much loss there, either. But we did have to start thinking about improving our levee system in case anything like that was ever to happen again."

The tabasco pepper fields on Avery Island are perhaps in one of the least vulnerable sites anywhere in Cajun Country, and yet a good portion of the acreage where they grow there is still vulnerable to flooding. And all the acreage is susceptible to high winds and torrential rains.

Oddly, these are not the most challenging conditions that Harold faces in trying to ensure that McIlhenny has enough tabasco peppers every year to satisfy its worldwide clientele. Shifting political conditions, coups, and dictatorships are on this list now. Tabasco peppers are primarily contract-grown at specially selected sites throughout Latin America, and have been since the mid-1960s. The fields left on Avery are reserved for the seed stock distributed to the contract growers in a handful of the Latin American countries chosen for their optimal quality. What has driven McIlhenny to place its peppers in other areas (that are politically less stable than the United States) is not the vulnerability of Avery Island to floods or hurricanes, but the declining workforce of Cajun Country, and the constant threat of attacks by new virus diseases and weevil pests wherever peppers are grown.

While riding the pepper boom in New Iberia, there were lots of folks making money growing and picking peppers. In Richard Schweid's book *Hot Peppers,* an exploration of Cajun culture and *Capsicum,* he reported that in 1978 a grower could gross about $3,750 an acre for tabasco peppers, which amounts to about $13,040.40 in 2010 dollars, or a veritable fortune in the eyes of most vegetable or grain farmers. However, historically the harvest was done with manual labor, with multiple passes and pickings. Meanwhile, other large US chile-growing regions like New Mexico and California have embraced technologies in the seeds and varieties that facilitate the use of mechanical harvesters. These regions grow varieties of *C. annuum* with larger sizes of pepper fruits—jalapeños or New Mexican stuffing chiles that are now approaching a foot in length. The smaller tabasco still ripens sporadically and unevenly—a calling card that signals just how little breeding has been done on it for conventional crop improvement—so it just doesn't jibe well with mechanical harvesting. During the domestication of other horticultural crops, larger fruit size was among the first changes that farmers selected for in order to shift from the wild version to a domesticated one.

At about the time that manual pepper-harvesting costs began to climb, the oil industry started to make waves in the region, offering unskilled laborers the chance at making better hourly wages rather than piecework wages picking crops. Pickers left Louisiana's fields in droves, becoming roustabouts on oil rigs, truck drivers, or pipe layers.

Harold was candid about the company's need to have options outside of Cajun Country: "Viruses and of course the availability of labor are now our biggest issues in deciding where we grow tabascos. But our problems sort of cycle; it's not necessarily the same issue in the same

place every year. True, some of our grow-out sites have risks that others
don't have. South of the Darién Gap [between Panama and Colombia],
there's no pepper weevils, but that used to be a pain to deal with at
our more northerly sites. We've had tobacco mosaic, cucumber mosaic,
potato virus Y. Some of these viruses are transmitted by thrips [a small
agricultural pest], others are carried by beetles, still others by whiteflies.
Now we're realizing that you can't visually ID everything, because you
can't assume it is just the symptoms of one virus, but multiple ones
might be present."

Harold went on, giving us a hint of how deeply he had thought
through these issues: "We don't think our strains of tabasco peppers have
ever been intentionally bred by us or by anyone else, but it seems that
they're somehow nematode-resistant. This may simply be due to our
visual selection of vigorous types, but not to intentional hybridization.
It's still essentially an heirloom, a land race with a good deal of variation
still observed in our fields. Is there much variation in the flavor of the
peppers grown from our seeds at different sites in Latin America? Sure,
to some extent: That's why we blend them for a more consistent product. But yes, you can definitely smell and taste the differences among
batches between sites, or even between years from the same site."

"But how do these potential threats play out in the way McIlhenny
manages its pepper production in Latin America?" Kraig asked Harold.

"We tend to run from viruses to reduce our risk. But there's always
a problem to deal with in our grow-outs in Latin America—aphids, a
tropical storm, a political coup . . . Nevertheless, we've continued on in
some of the same areas down there where we first worked years ago.
Some of our current growers are the grandkids of the first growers
whom we initially recruited."

When we sat down together, back at the office, we wanted to ask
Harold what we considered *the big question:* how Tabasco sauce has
managed to maintain the same taste of place—*terroir*—even though the
peppers themselves are produced in at least a dozen localities in half a
dozen countries. Harold had alluded to some controls that McIlhenny
has on the pepper quality: All the seed stock is produced on Avery Island

for dissemination to the other sites; all peppers are ground and the mash is mixed with Avery Island salt (also shipped with the seeds) and placed immediately in the same oak barrels; all peppers harvested from all the sites are "pooled" when they are returned to the island for processing.

Because of his background working in the salt-harvesting operation, when Harold thought about the *terroir* of Tabasco sauce, he did not stop at the taste of the peppers in isolation. He put up four fingers on his right hand as he began to explain: "There are four very different factors that work together in Tabasco: the peppers themselves, the salt from the salt domes here on Avery Island, the old-style grain vinegar that we use, and the oak wood barrels in which we do the fermentation and aging."

That surprised us all, because often *terroir* is simply stereotyped as the effects of climate or, alternatively, soil on the taste profiles of a crop like wine grapes. But Harold's experience suggested that the distinctive flavor of a particular pepper product is derived from a far more complex set of interactions.

"First, wherever we grow them in any particular year, we end up with millions of pounds of ripe, red, hand-selected tabasco peppers. They're all of the same historic strain, but they do harbor some genetic variation still. What I'm saying is that we haven't been able to detect that they're suffering in any way from inbreeding. After their harvest—in every country but Colombia, which won't let us bring it in—we pack all the peppers in salt from our own source here on the island.

"The interesting thing about this salt is that it has bigger granule sizes, almost like those of many kosher salts, but even those kosher salts have typically been redistilled. Our salt has not been out of solution since dinosaurs roamed the earth during the Jurassic period. To taste, it *seems* saltier, perhaps due to the largeness of its flakes, not just because of its chemical composition. We're low-sodium in our product, but the salt still gives it some of its flavor."

He paused and handed each of us some miniature bottles of Tabasco sauces. "Next, keep in mind that the mash of peppers and salt is wood-aged for three years. The new mash just doesn't ever taste like what we get after three years of aging in those Jack Daniel's whiskey barrels.

# Climate Change and Hurricanes

In the summer of 2005, Dr. Peter J. Webster of Georgia Tech submitted a very interesting article to *Science* magazine, the preeminent peer-reviewed academic journal. Titled "Changes in Tropical Cyclone Number, Duration, and Intensity in a Warming Environment,"* it was accepted for publication–a great honor for any scientist–on August 18, 2005. Dr. Webster's article was prescient on many levels. Five days later, Hurricane Katrina formed over the southeastern Bahamas, on its way to becoming the sixth most powerful Atlantic hurricane ever recorded, and the most costly in US history, causing over eighty-one billion dollars in damage, with more than eighteen hundred people losing their lives in the hurricane or the subsequent floods.

If climate change continues unabated, are these the type of extreme events we can come to expect? Dr. Webster and his team explored this question by looking at historical data on hurricanes in the major oceanic basins. Are there any signs of increase in the surface sea temperature over the last thirty-five years? Is there any change in the frequency or intensity of hurricanes in the major oceanic basins? Are these correlated? It is known that surface sea temperatures over twenty-six degrees Celsius (seventy-nine degrees Fahrenheit) are necessary for the formation and creation of tropical storms and hurricanes, and it is thought that the hotter the sea surface temperature when storms are formed, the greater their potential intensity. A sobering thought when we think about the predicted temperature rises for the next fifty-plus years.

What Dr. Webster and his colleagues discovered will not surprise anyone reading this book. There was a global increase in tropical ocean temperatures of 0.5 degree Celsius over the thirty-five-year period they studied. Additionally, they found that, while there was not an overall increase in the *abso-*

When it's new, it's a bit acrid, you know, acidic and somewhat fruity in flavor. The older it gets, it is less fruity, but a bit more yeasty and subtle. We're trying to figure out what it is that they're getting from that process, but we're still not sure, technically speaking. The fermentation process itself only takes six weeks, so maybe that's just a small part of the flavor-enhancing compared to the aging. And we continue to use beechwood-generated vinegar—not acetator vinegar as is used in nearly all other vinegar-based hot sauces. We get this older style of vinegar that takes weeks of exposure to the vinegar mother to ferment, rather than like the acetator vinegar that is only in with the mother culture for a few hours."

*lute number* of hurricanes globally, there was an increase in the number of hurricanes that reached category 4 and 5 strength–the highest intensities, with the greatest potential for major impacts to land and property, and typically loss of lives.

Dr. Webster followed this global paper with one in 2007** that looked only at data from the North Atlantic Ocean, which has had better data recording than the other oceanic regions. We'll let him report his findings in his own words:

> We find that long-period variations in tropical cyclone and hurricane frequency over the past century in the North Atlantic Ocean have occurred as three relatively stable regimes separated by sharp transitions. Each regime has seen 50% more cyclones and hurricanes than the previous regime and is associated with a distinct range of sea surface temperatures (SSTs) in the eastern Atlantic Ocean. Overall, there appears to have been a substantial 100-year trend leading to related increases of over 0.78 C in SST and over 100% in tropical cyclone and hurricane numbers. It is concluded that the overall trend in SSTs, and tropical cyclone and hurricane numbers is substantially influenced by greenhouse warming.

In other words, "aberrant" hurricane seasons like that of 2005, when Hurricanes Dennis, Katrina, Rita, and Wilma made themselves at home in the Gulf of Mexico, just might become closer to the norm for the foreseeable future.

Kraig

* P. J. Webster, G. J. Holland, J. A. Curry, and H.-R. Chang, "Changes in tropical cyclone number, duration, and intensity in a warming environment," *Science* (September 16, 2005): 1844-6.
** G. J. Holland and P. J. Webster, "Heightened tropical cyclone activity in the North Atlantic: natural variability or climate trend?" *Philosophical Transactions of Royal Society A* (2007): 2695-2716..

It was getting close to sunset, and the shadows from nearby shade trees were creeping in on our scene. Avery Island was stunningly beautiful, and Harold could see in our faces the recognition of that fact.

"I need to say this. Unlike the producers of hot sauces based on other kinds of chile peppers, *we can't just go out and buy tabascos someplace.* We grow our seed out *here,* plus do some research and development of growing practices that we hope to transfer to our other sites in Latin America as well. There are about five hundred acres of fields potentially available for grow-out on Avery Island, but we're down to using no more than fifty-seven acres in recent years. Actually, this year we grew out just twenty acres. About half of all our production is now under drip irrigation so that we can encourage our Latin American colleagues to conserve water wherever they can . . ."

Harold paused, and got a thoughtful look on his rather expressive face and its five o'clock shadow. It was then, at the very the end of our visit with Harold Osborn, that he quietly stated the most interesting principle guiding McIlhenny's relationship with this heirloom pepper.

"You see, the main issue that guides us is this: *How we live and work here on Avery Island is ultimately about long-term conservation.* If we soil our own nest here, it will come back to haunt us, our cousins, our children. So that's why we're always thinking about the potential consequences of our actions—everything from our consumption to our management practices—not just how they'll affect the bottle line over the short term, but how they may play out over several generations.

"I mean, keep this in mind: We've now been managing this island as Averys and McIlhennys for nine generations, and if you count the kids coming up, we've been here for eleven generations, or almost 200 years."

We thanked Harold, and he bid us good-bye. It was just past sunset when we got the Spice Ship over to the toll bridge where we left the microcosm of Avery Island behind, to return to the world at large. We hightailed it for New Orleans, hoping to catch Louis Michot's band at the Hi-Ho Lounge when they started at nine. Fortunately, we arrived a little after eight, in time to have a beer with Louis and hear him weave out his dreams in a charming Cajun accent.

Louis is not only a musician and folklorist, but a cultural conservationist who has worked with the Cultural Resource Institute of Acadiana on various projects. He began to spin out his plans for an heirloom vegetable seed bank to serve Cajun families throughout Acadiana, in case they ever need an Ark like Noah did, and also to promote older heritage varieties of vegetables that are being lost. But before we got too deep into the conversation, the others in the Lost Bayou Ramblers summoned him up to the stage to do their sound checks.

While we waited for their performance, we got to speculating again about the band's name, the Lost Bayou Ramblers, and their CD title,

*Bayou Perdu.* Why *that* name, at *this* point in time? What does a young Cajun man like Louie see as at risk of being lost? The wherewithal to ramble? The chance to drive back into the old fields and orchards and settlements due to the coastal erosion and widening of the bayou channels, or the bayous themselves, as they are starved of the sediments that once nourished them, and scoured by storms that transform them into open bays?

Then the band's own music started up and flooded the Hi-Ho. As we watched Louis, his brother, and his friends play, we felt their fervor. It was not that they played with a sense of desperation or foreboding, but there was something there that viscerally acknowledged what may be their ultimate motivation: If you don't play your heart out while you can, something might otherwise be lost, something deep and cultural, familial, and at the root of all you stand upon and stand for.

Alan LeFleur, the upright bass player, flung off his jacket, stripped down to his undershirt, stocking cap, and jeans, leaned the huge wooden instrument at a forty-five-degree angle off the floor, and slapped it like he was bringing someone or something back to life after a near-drowning. Cavan Carruth, the rhythm guitarist, bald and muscular, shed his shirt and hat as well, and strummed the guitar with the ferocity of a man pulling the cord on an old chain saw. Chris Courville, the drummer, pounded on his snare as if the beat he was making must work to scare away all the demons.

Louis's brother André—the dark, curly-haired man with the squeezebox—pumped his arms like he was using it to blow up a giant life raft. And Louis himself flailed away at his fiddle, rocking and twisting his torso as though the sheer trancelike magic of his mesmerizing melodies might be able to turn back the floods, hold down the surging sea levels, and keep Cajun French from ever being lost from the tongues of his own children and their grandchildren to come.

The audience—if you want to call them that, for they were not passive listeners but participants in the same trance—responded in kind. As they spun around together on the Hi-Ho's small dance floor, they clung to one another's shoulders, waists, and butts as if for dear life. They would roar and clap every time Louis Michot ended a two-step or waltz with an earsplitting Cajun catcall, and jump up and down every time they glimpsed the bassist and guitarist leaping into the air.

This was more than idle entertainment, aerobic exercise, or cultural appreciation. This was a cathartic affirmation that if the land and the people were to survive, someone damn well better act like all this mattered. Or it all might wash away.

# New England Clam Chowder

At first this recipe may seem like an odd selection for a book about chiles, but it's included here for a simple reason: It is the one dish that truly benefits the most from the addition of Tabasco sauce.

The heady aroma, the rich, creamy broth, the deep, succulent clam flavor—they're all enhanced by just a couple of dashes of the original version of Tabasco. It speaks well of the ubiquity of the little red bottles that you are likely to find them on the table at just about any ramshackle New England clam shack.

Like so many other dishes, chowder takes its name from the pot it is prepared in. Or, more accurately, it takes its name from the French name for the pot it's cooked in: *chaudier*. To completely Anglicize it, though, its correct pronunciation within the six New England states is CHOW-dah.

An authentic chowder would of course be made with fresh clams. In fact, in Rhode Island a very specific clam is called for—the official state shellfish, the quahog (pronounced KO-hog). Despite the odd name, it is in fact a large, hard-shell clam and not a pig. Nevertheless, in this recipe we use canned clams purely for convenience and accessibility. To use fresh instead, simply steam open about 6 pounds of cherrystone (or other) clams, strain and reserve the liquor, and shell and chop the clams. Then proceed with the rest of the recipe.

1 large yellow onion, diced
1½ pounds red potatoes, diced
2 stalks celery, diced
1 tablespoon stemmed and chopped fresh thyme
2½ teaspoons sage
1 teaspoon white pepper
½ cup (4 ounces) butter

**¼ cup flour**

**3 pounds canned clams, with juice (that's about 12 of those little cans)**

**1 pint buttermilk**

Sauté the onion, potatoes, celery, thyme, sage, and white pepper in the butter in a large stockpot over medium-high heat until the vegetables are tender. Stir in the flour and reduce the heat to medium. Add the clams and their juice. Bring to a simmer and continue simmering for about 15 minutes, stirring frequently (watch out for scorching). Stir in the buttermilk, reheat, then serve immediately with crusty bread and plenty of Tabasco sauce on the side. *Serves 6-8.*

# CHAPTER FIVE

# Strings of Chiles Like Rosary Beads Along the Rio Grande

**THERE WAS ICE** packed against the ridges of the Sangre de Cristo Mountains, lazy curls of fragrant cedar smoke rising from the chimneys of nearly every adobe home, and snow-dusted chamisa bushes shining in the last light of day along the sides of the icy roads. We had arrived in the only place in the nation that has an official state question, one that most residents could answer at breakfast time in any truck stop or coffee shop, even if it still continued to dumbfound all the newcomers:

"Red or green?"

Chile sauce, that is—the perennial subject of the New Mexico state question. All three of us gastronauts have a warm spot in our hearts and bellies for the native foods and small farms nestled along the Upper Rio Grande watershed of northern New Mexico. Kraig had spent parts of his impetuous youth there, sowing his wild chiles on the outskirts of Albuquerque, where he first experimented with spicy foods and developed quite the chile habit. Kurt spent the summer of 1985 as an intern in Santa Fe, and he and his wife, Kim, regularly take refuge there in the winter as part of the Edible Institute and to take part in an editors' rendezvous for the *Edible* magazines (regional local-food magazines under the *Edible* umbrella) like their own in the Iowa River Valley. And Gary has many dear old friends and Lebanese kin scattered around Santa Fe, where clan members of his in-laws once ran the Kelly-Gross Trading Posts that marketed native New Mexican chiles, pinyon nuts, and sheep hides to Navajos, Anglos, and Hispanics alike. It was the perfect place for the Spice Ship to hover for a few days in the winter of 2010.

Perhaps no other state in the Union—if not all of the Americas, from Alaska south to Tierra del Fuego—has a higher percentage of residents who link their cultural identity to the daily consumption of *Capsicum annuum*. More chile peppers are grown in the fields irrigated by the nineteen hundred miles of the Rio Grande—from San Juan and Hinsdale Counties in Colorado to El Paso and Hudspeth Counties in Texas and across the border in Chihuahua, Mexico—than in the rest of the North America.

For now, though, the deep snows were blanketing the high sierra, and New Mexico did not feel like a "hot spot." Massive snow clouds were lunging toward us on the western horizon and flurries had begun to obscure our view of the Sangre de Cristos behind us, forcing us into the same kind of uncertain weather that many of the farmers we had been interviewing faced every month.

Apparently, an El Niño year had begun to heap much-needed moisture on the arid region, breaking a drought that had nearly reached the epic proportions of the Dust Bowl days of the 1930s and Larry McMurtry's *Last Picture Show* era of the 1950s. What that immediately meant to us was that our original plans might be scrambled by the ever-more-unpredictable weather of the semi-arid Southwest.

And so we gathered around a fireplace in one of the great rooms at the Bishop's Lodge in Tesuque, while the juniper logs that stoked the fire offered up the familiar "cedar" fragrance like an incense. We took time out to get caught up with one another, reporting on our recent solo excursions.

"So you were able to get down past Albuquerque to Isleta Pueblo?" Kraig asked Gary. "I used to know the South Valley pretty well, but it seems more and more urbanized every time I see it. Are there many commercial chile growers left down that way?"

"I don't think there are *many* . . . ," Gary replied, fumbling for his note-pad in a blue jean jacket pocket. "My friend Shawn Kelley took me to Isleta to see Joseph Jaramillo, owner of a traditional foods micro-enterprise called Native and Natural. The Jaramillo family gets a few food products from their Native American neighbors, but most years Joseph grows all the chiles he sells . . . Let me find the notes I took while we were buying some of his place-based heritage products . . . Oh, here it is . . . let me read you a bit of Mr. Jaramillo's commentaries that he offered at his store:

"'At Isleta Pueblo these days, I think I'm the only one still commer-cially growing chiles. I have twelve acres to work with, and although I do most of it myself, I try to involve the youth around here whenever I can . . .'"

"Twelve acres is a lot to hand-harvest!" Kurt responded. "My wife, Kim, tried to manage just a few acres for our restaurant two summers ago and she about wore herself out."

"Well, I'm not saying it's easy for Mr. Jaramillo," Gary said. "He has weeds and pests and heat to deal with, and it's tough getting the timing of his irrigations just right for each crop he sows. But it's been his lifework, a dream that he hasn't been able to shake since he was just a youngster helping harvest his father's fields. Listen how Mr. Jaramillo described that dream:

"'I've been involved with farming ever since I was a kid. When I was young, I would take a good look at all the vegetables we grew and think to myself, this is just awesome. Fat melons. Huge chiles. It was just amazing. It was something I wanted to be engaged with, not just while I was young, but for the rest of my life.'"

Kraig grinned. "I know what he means. Harvest time is an absolutely magical time on the farm. Add to that the smell of roasting chile every fall—that's a dream I wouldn't want to wake up from."

"So what kind of chile peppers does he grow?" Kurt asked.

"Joseph's own words describe them . . . Let me see where I scribbled that down . . . Oh, here it is:

"'Well, I've tried to stay with two types of our native [Isleta] chiles all along. One is long and has broad shoulders. The other Isleta chile is shorter, but is still good. But it's been about ten years now—at least from 1998 to 2008—that I've had difficulty getting really good-quality chiles out of my fields. Compared to what we grew in those days, the Isleta chile today is a lot different than what it was back then . . . I guess that our native chile has been mixed up with others. There are so many varieties and people here just plant their seeds, any old seeds, without knowing where they originated and whether they're adapted.'"

At this point, Kraig was practically bursting at the seams. He saw an opportunity to tie together ideas regarding the origin and establishment of northern New Mexican heirlooms, the degradation of those local lines just as Mr. Jaramillo had observed, and the potential risks of accidental cross-pollination of chiles. And so, like a jazz musician, he began an improvisational weaving of many facts and stories into one as we sat transfixed by both the story and the fire.

"Northern New Mexico," Kraig reminded us, "has more named varieties of heirloom chile peppers than the rest of the United States combined. At the very same time that chile peppers were brought back to the Old World by Spanish shipping fleets, the Spaniards introduced other chiles northward into New Mexico as they continued to search for gold and riches. It appears that the ancestors of the chile peppers Mr. Jaramillo grows came up the trade route known as El Camino Real. Now, the Camino Real was developed to help the Spanish extract mineral wealth from New Mexico, sending colonists, missionaries, and supplies north, and sending silver to the south. Along with these supplies came crops not grown in the region previously—barley, wheat, peas, fruit trees, and, of course, chiles."

Kraig was jazzed, so he continued. "Although there's good evidence of pre-Hispanic contact between the New Mexican pueblos and indigenous groups farther south, in present-day Mexico there are no indications of pre-Hispanic use of chile peppers north of the border. The closest place chiles were definitely found prior to the Spanish settlement of New Mexico was near Casas Grandes, Chihuahua, less than a hundred miles south of the current international borderline.

"But here's the kicker . . ." Kraig took a deep breath and continued. "The heirloom chiles historically and currently grown in New Mexico have since become so distinct from those in surrounding states that they have their own pod type! What's a *pod type*? It's a horticultural division within a species like *Capsicum annuum*. In other words, varieties within the same species are grouped together into roughly defined types based on the shapes of their fruit. New Mexican chiles have a such a peculiar form compared with the rest of the heap that they were given their own particular category.

"The original chile cultivated along the Rio Grande likely had a pod that was modestly long—about four or five inches—broad-shouldered, and thick-fleshed. It was grown for dual purposes: to be eaten when green, probably for stuffing like a *chile relleno,* or to be dried in the sun. That's when it turns blood red and dries into a brittle, leathery commodity that can be stored for months. And then, whenever you need it, it can be reconstituted into a rich reddish brown *chile colorado.* That thinner sauce can be seasoned with salt, white pepper, a couple of cloves of garlic, and oil or pork lard, then thickened with cornstarch or cornmeal for enchilada sauce."

It still wasn't entirely clear for Kurt. "I still don't get how much difference there really is among all these New Mexican pod types from different pueblos."

Kraig passed the baton off to Gary, as if they were in a relay race. "Go for it, old man."

"Thanks a lot . . . just remember, I've been eating chiles for as long as you've been out of diapers! And what you just asked, Kurt, is a key question, but it can't be answered merely with the eyes and the left side of the brain. The differences lie in how the chiles grow in different climes and how they taste. Over the last four hundred years, each Native American pueblo and most Hispanic communities in the Upper Rio Grande have adapted a variant of this 'native chile' to their own soils, water sources, and growing seasons. And as a chef, you can probably guess that they also selected them for their suitability for different uses. Different ethnic groups wanted different culinary qualities in their chiles: textures, colors, heat levels, capacity to absorb liquids, suitability for stuffing when fresh and green or for making a sauce when dried and reddened. And, of course, different folks desired different levels of piquancy. So now all these pueblos have their own place-based name for their local heirloom: San Juan, Española, Chimayó, El Guique, Nambé, Velarde, Isleta, Escondida, Santo Domingo, Jarales, Embudo, Alcaldé, San Felipé, Jemez, Cochiti, and Zia."

"Compared with your learned lecture a couple of minutes ago, Dr. Kraft," Kurt said, grinning, "the elderly Dr. Nabhan here sounds like a walking New Mexican phone book! That was a pretty good geography lesson, old man. So are there still more than a dozen distinct place-based varieties of native New Mexican chiles, or are those days long gone?"

Kraig took back the baton. "They're fading fast, for the very reasons that Mr. Jaramillo was getting at. The problem is that, with the declining number of growers for each of these types, each population or variety of chile has fewer and fewer plants out in the field, reducing the genetic diversity in each. This reduction in genetic diversity leads to less fit individuals, biologically speaking. In other words, they lack the genetic background that would enable them to deal with changing conditions, either from pests or from the weather. This contributes to the phenomenon that Mr. Jaramillo told Gary about—that for several years his same seed lot kept delivering an ever-more-meager yield. That's because chiles are predominantly self-pollinating, so if you keep a small population, you slowly lose diversity in your population and accumulate bad traits.

"In contrast, traditional chile farmers in central Mexico know this and bring in seeds from other pueblos to renew or revive their seed lots through crossing and then subsequent selection of the chiles they like. On the other hand, if you start planting commercial varieties of chiles nearby—say, the NuMex hybrids—you may have accidental crosses that are not intended and that may dilute the heirloom genetics. It is really a balancing act—a careful management of the population on a communal level that helps maintain the vigor and yield of any heirloom chile variety."

When Kraig finished his lecture, he looked up at Gary and Kurt to see if they'd followed all of the steps in his logic.

"I get it—it narrows the gene pool, like royal inbreeding. But just what makes one of these heirloom chiles hotter and taste different than these other chiles?" Kurt asked Kraig and Gary.

Kraig grinned again. "Do you want another ten-minute explanation, one involving genetics and environment and their interactions, or do you want a more succinct answer from a farmer? The short answer is genetics and stress, and I think most farmers will have their own explanation that points back to that."

Gary nodded. "It seems that every New Mexican chile farmer has his own answer to this one. Listen to what Mr. Jaramillo told us.

"'What makes chiles hotter one year more than another? Even here at Isleta, you'll have different opinions from different gardeners and former farmers, but the one I agree with is that it depends on how you control the water reaching your plants over the entire season. The trouble is, you have to be able to predict weather conditions to some extent to know just when to flood-irrigate. You schedule it to let the plants get dry. Once they're starting to mature, the first pick of the peppers will not be as hot as later ones. The second pick will tend to be hotter, or whatever it's gonna be. You gotta keep it dry or the chiles will get way too hot.'"

Gary looked up from his notes. "At this point I asked Mr. Jaramillo if he meant the chiles might get too *spicy* hot to eat, or too *stressed* by temperatures in his field. I think his answer hints that something is happening to the local microclimates around here:

"'Actually, a little bit of shading will really help the chile plant keep its cool,' Mr. Jaramillo replied. 'If it's hot weather, it really helps for them to be in the shady area under trees on the edge of the field. The hottest days during a drought will stress the chiles. That's how I was motivated to explore this shade concept last summer. The excessive heat really got my attention last year. But I used to believe otherwise, that chiles were sort of desert plants, that they could take the heat. Keep in mind that when I was first farming over twenty years ago, all the farmers around

# New Mexican Native Chile

## (Capsicum annuum)

Ahh . . . New Mexican chile. I can't think about it and not salivate. Although I spent my formative years in New Mexico, I had no idea then of the importance that chile peppers would come to have in my life. Now that the chile pepper has become the object of my research and the focus of the last five years of my life, I realize that it all started with green and red chiles in New Mexico.

After I moved with my family to New Mexico as an eight-year-old, my culinary palate didn't stray too far from either Filipino or "classic" American fare. My Filipina mother adapted to life in the United States by learning to cook all the classic American dishes–all the more to help us children assimilate after spending the first years of our life abroad in the Philippines and Greece. After meat loaf, chicken potpie, adobo, pancit, and spaghetti and meatballs, I wasn't quite ready for a

world bathed in red or green chile sauce. But sooner or later, it happens to all of us who have lived in New Mexico. You come to realize that your eggs, burgers, or pizzas just aren't the same without it.

Walk into any major fast-food joint or chain restaurant in New Mexico and you will find New Mexican chiles. Every McDonald's has a double cheeseburger with green chiles on the menu, and Pizza Hut has green chiles as a topping. In fact, in all of New Mexico, a pepperoni pizza just isn't ordered without green chiles, unless it's for a little kid's birthday party.

Becoming enamored with New Mexican chile has all the earmarks of chemical addiction. You find yourself at New Mexican restaurants more often, "experimenting" with green or red chiles on different types of dishes–perhaps this time you'll try green

here used to advise me to never grow chile plants in or near the shade of trees. Now that's something I more or less have to do—to keep them from getting direct sun all day long—'"

"That's pretty interesting, given the urban heat island forming around Albuquerque," Gary said, interrupting the reading of his notes. "They say that cities in the Southwest are heating up far faster than the global warming trends predict, in part because they have so many roofs and paved streets and parking lots. Albuquerque is just up the road from the Jaramillo farm, and it devotes more space to paved parking lots than to any other single land use in the metropolitan area! Kraig, do you remember that Australian science paper I sent you about chiles and solar radiation a while back? It argues that in most places chiles not with that stuffed *sopapilla*. Maybe you'll even feel a bit bold and try both sauces, ordering your *huevos rancheros* "Christmas-style." Soon, at the grocery store, you start buying cans of Hatch chile, and finding that, while it serves in a pinch and in certain circumstances, it just doesn't have the same punch as what you had at Mary and Tito's Café, at Los Cuates, at Sadie's, or even in that breakfast burrito you bought at the street corner. In your desire to recapture that feeling, that taste and sensation, you'll go to the source and skip the middleman. In the fall, independent chile roasters occupy the corners of parking lots and appear in vacant lots at stoplights. Even Walmart will have chile roasting in the parking lot. The large barrel roasters are clearly visible, and they lace the air with the intoxicating smell of roasting green chiles, much like chumming the waters, to lure in all the chile addicts. At this point, your Pavlovian response is all but assured. You'll pull over and buy a bushel to tide you over.

Late September comes along and you are getting anxious. Where is your next fix coming from? Harvest time is ending! Don't worry about being stuck without. Roasted green chile is easily frozen, losing neither quality nor flavor. And if you prefer the red? Well, that's dried and bagged or strung into *ristras*. You'll have enough of both to last you through the winter, spring, and summer. Provided you can monitor yourself and mete out your dosage.

What's that you say? Never tried it before? Well, you should just go on to New Mexico and try some yourself. First time is always free . . .

Kraig

only grow best in partial shade, but their canopy is designed to be self-shading to reduce the effects of damaging radiation . . ."

"Yeah, I remember—it's much like the chiltepin, the wild progenitor. All of this is true—the need for some shade in the extreme climates and the extreme use of parking lots in Albuquerque. In California, my wife and my friends constantly joke that I never learned to park a car properly because I learned to drive in Albuquerque and never had to parallel-park—because there were always open spots in the parking lot! In high school, we would spend some restless nights hanging out in parking lots—even playing ultimate Frisbee under the lights. But I also agree with Mr. Jaramillo and the *Science* article about too much sun for chile peppers. The sun cuts both ways: Too much direct sun on the fruits causes physical damage—sunburns or sun scorch—and while the plants need the sun, they don't want too much of it.

"As an Iowa boy, I guess I should be glad I'm here in the middle of the winter," Kurt added. "We have a whole different kind of hot up there, but it's not the glaring, arid heat of the desert. Then again, even these deep snows are nothing like an Iowa winter. When I left to come down here, it was minus twenty-nine Fahrenheit. In seven months, it'll be ninety-eight, with a 98 percent humidity to match."

Kurt was eager to talk about his excursion northward from the warm fires of Tesuque. "We just came back from the little mountain village of Chimayó, where Kim and I found a fantastic little place and the best tamales I've ever had."

What Kurt and Kim had found was Léona's, a modest little *restaurante* nestled beside the holy shrine of Santuario de Nuestro Señor de Esquipulas. "It started as a roadside stand," Kurt explained. "As a girl, Léona Medina-Tiede used to help her uncle prepare and serve posole and tortillas to the hungry pilgrims during Holy Week. She loved the work and eventually built a little stand of her own. That stand got enclosed, then expanded, and expanded again until it had been literally built around a massive catalpa tree that provides beautiful decor inside, and shade for the roof from the desert sun.

"The place is still a family affair, with Léona's kids helping out. Alongside the tamales, which had Chimayó chiles actually mixed into the *masa* [the corn dough that surrounds the filling of a tamale], they also serve her uncle's posole, *carne adovada,* burritos, chili stew, frito pies, nachos, and *biscochitos*." Kurt paused for a moment with that far-off look in his eye that Kraig and Gary had become accustomed to, the one he gets when he's lost in a daydream about some favorite meal.

Gary nudged him back to the present. Kurt continued, "Yeah, so they serve mostly takeout, but there are a few tables, and most of the menu is available to be shipped, next-day air, anywhere you want it. You can bet I'll be keeping my home freezer fully stocked."

With visions of tamales still dancing in his head, Kurt needed to know more about what Kraig had been eating now that he'd returned to his old stomping grounds. "Kraig, have you gotten your necessary dose of chiles since arriving at your folks' place in Albuquerque?"

"Since I left New Mexico for school," Kraig answered, my folks have always been sending me care packages of roasted green chiles from their garden, so they know how I need to get my fill while I'm there. We went to a quintessential New Mexican place, Mary and Tito's Café— they've been operating for almost fifty years. Simple, unadorned food. The *carne adovada* was absolutely amazing—the red chile was smoky and with enough heat to burn it to your memory."

"I can't stand it any longer," Gary moaned. "I need another dose of chiles myself to stave off all this cold. Let's all hop into the Spice Ship and drive down to the Santa Fe Farmer's Market before the snow forces road closures . . ."

When we arrived at the farmer's market, not far from where the old Kelly-Gross bodega stands on the edge of the railroad yard, there were few cars that had braved the cold out in the parking lot. But inside the new building, constructed to keep the farmer's market alive all year long, there were still a number of die-hard farmers and artisans hawking their wares. Some sold chile pepper seedlings to keep inside until the last frost had passed. Others sold ornamental chile wreaths, while a few Hispanic families sold plastic bags and sacks of freshly ground chile powder, as well as the cracked chile pods known as *chile caribe*. And then we spotted the tables of newly dried chile pods and garlic that were being tended by one of the most tenacious farmers at the market, Matt Romero.

In Santa Fe, some restaurants no longer advertise that they use *local* chiles in their recipes, for that word has become hackneyed and diluted by repackaged products from afar. What they do note on their menus, blackboards, and marquees is that they feature Matt Romero's chiles from nearby Dixon, not too far up the Rio Grande. Matt, once a chef himself, simply knows what chefs and home cooks are looking for in peppers. And he provides them to his devoted customers year-round, snow or no snow, heat or no heat.

When Matt Romero shows his hand-selected chiles to the faithful
who line up at his booth, their mouths begin to water, their eyes tear
up, and their eyes look off into the distance, as if a gorgeous rainbow
were breaking out across the sky. As Matt once put it to Santa Fe writer
Amy Traverso, "My chiles have nice, big, thick shoulders . . . The flavor
is incredible, with quite a bit of heat. Describing it is like trying to
describe sex. Words are just sometimes not adequate."

When we arrived at his market booth, Matt was cheerfully carrying
on three conversations with his customers at once, loading their shopping bags with plastic sacks full of dried red chile pods. Even though
the cold outside was leaking into the farmer's market pavilion, Matt
wore only a light gray sweatshirt, a colorful orange-and-purple apron
promoting the Santa Fe Farmer's Market (whose advisory board he
serves on), a sweat-stained ballcap, a faded pair of blue jeans, and some
muddy boots. Although his hair and goatee are peppered with gray,
there is something about Romero that makes him seem forever young,
as if his intense interest in the green and growing world has staved off
aging. He wears glasses, yet you immediately notice how his eyes light
up whenever he talks about chiles, and that it seems he can stay on that
topic all day long.

When Gary asked him about what his former life as a chef brings to
his work as a farmer and marketer, he offered a simple, upbeat answer:
"I think I have an eye and a sense of flavor for what people really like,
and that includes just what peppers can actually be *featured* on a restaurant menu. Chefs want chiles that are straight, not curled [the curled
ones are tough to stuff], with colorful skins and meaty flesh. I do watch
what high-end restaurants are doing with my chiles, but in the end the
restaurant trade gets what I have left *after* my farmer's market sales. This
is my most allegiant base. And that's because I offer them quality, variety,
and seasonality through all the various vegetables I grow."

We had sampled some of his small Japanese peppers stuffed with
goat cheese and topped with caviar at a local bar, but we knew that his
pride and joy was an older chile that had been part of his own family's
cultural legacy.

"Mostly, I'm growing the very same chile that my uncle Arthur Mendoza grew. He should be called the grandfather of 'Alcalde Improved'. It's a variety related to a New Mexico State University release by Frank Matta and Roy Nakayama from a couple of decades back. Up at the Espanola Valley Branch Experiment Field Station, just down the road from us, they took a great local chile—a really classic native New Mexican red chile—and crossed it to 'Sandia' to get a larger plant size and more pepper conformity. But before the station released 'Espanola Improved'—what they thought was the best progeny of their cross—they gave my uncle some of the other seeds to come out of their crosses. He took them and selected them not only for heat, but for tastiness and conformity—you know . . . straightness of the pod so that they're good stuffers for *rellenos*. Since then, our family has grown them continuously, every year, selecting them for other characteristics as well. Yield, ease of peeling the waxy skins of the pods, profuse branches, double flowers in every crotch of the branches, and blunt tips that are broad like a closed knuckle—those kinds of traits. So that's why we call it 'Alcalde Improved', though you could say it's a family heirloom."

"Where do you farm them?" Kraig asked.

"Oh, we have three different plots on farms around Embudo—you know, Dixon area—and Alcalde. The weather up there has been variable lately, but we adapt. We normally used to plant the first of May, but now it may be four or five days later to ensure that we don't get hit by a late frost. Fortunately, we've never lost an entire crop to a late frost. In fact I've seen our chile seedlings survive light frosts—can you imagine that?

"But up at our elevation, there's never too much hot weather for chiles—it just doesn't ever get as warm here as it does down near Albuquerque or Hatch. If we have to cut back the water we give them, the soil heats up to some extent, and then the meatiness of the chile pod is not as thick, and the yield in pounds diminishes. So when we have it, we water every other row every four days."

Gary then asked the obvious question: "You've just gone through a decade of drought, and the cities around here want more of the farmers' water to fuel their population growth. So they've begun to cut back the amount of water farmers may use. How have you dealt with that?"

Matt smiled, and soon we realized that it was a smile of relief: "We're just so fortunate, because our acequia has the most senior rights in our entire watershed, to the point that if the Rio Grande were gradually going dry, we would still get whatever irrigation water could be made available. Some of our acequias have been in more or less continuous use for three hundred to four hundred years.

"But it's not that we have reason to be lax about water. We actually do a lot of things to improve moisture-holding capacity of our soils—I compost heavily with green manures and always have. I've been farming the same ground for nine years, and rotate crops across it every three years."

Matt Romero was correct that his ditch community had senior rights for water during times of drought and scarcity, but he undoubtedly knew that this was a hard-won sanction to traditional chile farmers. For over five hundred years, these farmers have been distributing irrigation water through acequias, communally managed and operated open-air canals and ditches. Thanks to the tireless work of the New Mexico Acequia Association over the last quarter century, the irrigation rights of many farming families living along the rivers and streams have been safeguarded, at least for the immediate future.

Yet no farmers in the Rio Grande watershed can predict how water scarcity might affect them and their chile crops in the future, so none of them sleeps easy at night, or goes through a workday worry-free. The uncertainty plagues many farmers like Joe Gallegos, who irrigates his crops with water guaranteed by the senior rights of the San Luis People's Ditch in the headwater of the Rio Grande. Gallegos told water activist Katey Byrd that he still worries about this, even though he knows that his acequia "ditch crew" has always faced climatic variability ever since his great-great-grandfather Dario Gallegos helped dig the People's Ditch in 1852.

"Acequias are well designed to deal with drought," Joe Gallegos explained to Katey. "We live in a high-altitude desert, so we deal with drought almost every year. We have wet cycles and dry cycles. Drought has always been an issue with acequias . . . [but] as far as what global warming is going to do to us—I don't know how we're going to handle that."

The reason that Rio Grande farmers are facing unprecedented uncertainty is that the potential effects of climate change are likely to be exacerbated by political decisions regarding the amounts of water to be allotted to cities versus wildlife versus food production. In August 2007, New Mexico's state water engineer, John D'Antonio, asserted, "The Southwest United States is expected to be one of the five areas in the world that, over the next couple of decades, is going to receive less precipitation overall."

Because of this "expectation" or projection, New Mexico politicians have begun to ask a climate change advisory group—comprising scientists and engineers like D'Antonio—to help them chart a course for reducing societal risks to climate change. To begin, state agency personnel prepared an initial evaluation, released in 2005, that must have sobered any chile farmer reading it, especially any who had sought it out hoping for a *more* predictable future. The report suggested that, if no significant measures were soon taken to mitigate climate change, New Mexico would be facing a six- to twelve-degree Fahrenheit rise in air temperatures by the mid- to late twenty-first century. If air temperatures do indeed reach these heights, they would inevitably trigger dramatic changes in growing season length, snowpack melting, and the seasonal availability of river water for irrigation agriculture. The changes would be particularly severe in the mountain valleys at higher elevations in the state, such as those where the heirlooms known as Alcalde Improved, Chimayó, El Guique, Española, Jemez, San Juan, and Velarde continue to be grown.

In short, the report suggested that farmers in the state may suffer seasonal shortages of water, and would certainly face larger year-to-year variations in precipitation and water storage in reservoirs. In El Niño years in particular, it warned farmers of greater drought risks, because of

# Do Farmers Believe Climate Change Is Worth Shifting For?

As the climate change debate raged over the last fifteen years, agriculture was seen by some as a driver of climate change, while others asserted that sustainable agricultural practices could actually slow or reverse the rate of change. Also, it appeared to some observers that most farmers were skeptical of, if not downright antagonistic to, the notion that they should shift their practices to reduce greenhouse emissions associated with food production and transport.

American Farm Bureau Federation president Bob Stallman was one of those who weighed in, and he came out swinging.

"At the very time we need to increase our food production, climate change legislation threatens to slash our ability to do so," Stallman claimed in a January 2010 keynote address to his members. He argued that proposed legislation for climate change mitigation would shift as much as fifty-nine million acres of food production into tree crops and forestry, taking the equivalent of eight states' arable lands out of annual food crops to foster carbon sequestration via woody perennials. He warned:

> The world will continue to depend on food from the United States. To throttle back our ability to produce food–at a time when the United Nations projects billions of more mouths to feed–is a moral failure.

However, not all farming and ranching organizations in the United States agreed with Stallman's rhetoric, logic, or data. Other groups, such as the Rural Voices for Conservation Coalition (RVCC), wrote Senators John Kerry and Joe Lieberman this message:

> We strongly believe that a solution to the climate crisis is necessary, and that

greater anticipated evaporative loss from these reservoirs—particularly those in the Rio Grande watershed—and from crop plants themselves. Because snowpack would, on average, melt earlier, farmers would likely witness earlier spring runoff running by their fields as well as reduced flows through their acequias during the peak water demand periods of chiles and other irrigated crops.

Nevertheless, anyone who knows where and when water flows in the Southwest is well aware that climatic drought and water scarcity are often magnified by political decisions and economic pressures. Because

Americans must play a significant role in reducing greenhouse gas emissions. We believe that a solution can provide an opportunity for rural Americans to derive new sources of revenue from responsible stewardship and restoration.

While they voiced concerns about "how climate change will impact rural communities," their concerns were much different than those expressed by the Farm Bureau's national leadership. The coalition's farmers and ranchers recognized that the federal legislative proposals on climate were "a step forward in recognizing the importance of rural communities in addressing the anticipated impacts for climate change . . . and [implementing] strategies for emission reductions."

Another organization, the Family Farm Alliance, has had climate change as one of its priority issues since 2007. It is concerned that water scarcity caused by reduced rainfall and snowpack in the Intermountain West will decrease the amount of irrigation water avail-

able to vegetable growers as well as ranchers. It argues that using available water to ensure food security and self-sufficiency should become a national priority, and that the loss of farmlands, particularly near the most reliable water sources, should be curtailed.

Chile pepper farmers throughout the United States and Mexico have discussed with us their perceptions of how increasingly severe drought, water shortages, heat waves, storms, and floods have been affecting their food production. Although few of them attribute all of these meteorological events to global climate change, many do feel the shifting weather patterns have played a contributing role in the disasters they have suffered. Few of them waste much time arguing about the causes of these weather shifts, instead focusing their efforts on effective responses. Rather than behaving as helpless victims, most farmers we know are actively taking steps to reduce their future vulnerability to such events.

Gary

urban water uses in the Rio Grande basin are projected to double within the next half century even as natural water flows are anticipated to decline, we might say that the real challenge before chile farmers is a *political drought*—that is, the unwillingness of most politicians to honor the senior water rights of traditional acequia farmers if there are more votes to be gained by shunting some of that water to the more numerous voters living in metropolitan areas.

The New Mexican government is beginning to recognize the historical rights of the acequia, bit by bit. In April 2009, Governor Bill

Richardson signed bill HB 40, which limited the powers of municipalities to condemn water rights (basically a version of eminent domain for water rights), elevating the rights of acequias or other irrigation communities above the reach of municipalities, which must now negotiate their water on the market.

However, farmers and urban users are not the only water consumers. If the choice before New Mexicans was simply that between using water for pepper production and food security versus urban growth and recreation, the issue would be relatively cut-and-dried. But the Rio Grande was historically blessed with a good number of native fish, many of which are now at risk in the Rio Grande because the over-allocation of stream water for urban and agricultural uses leaves little left for any fish, at least for ones that wish to swim long distance and reproduce. The Rio Grande still does have some stretches with perennial flows, but they are shorter and shorter in length, and fewer and farther between.

This does not bode well for certain endangered fish such as the Rio Grande silvery minnow, which once ran from Española clear down to the Gulf of Mexico. Large-scale irrigation diversions from the Upper Rio Grande began in the 1880s, and a series of major dams, as well as four hundred miles of drains, were later constructed between Cochiti and Elephant Butte Lake in southern New Mexico. These manipulations of the Rio Grande drove the silvery minnow into decline, and some conservation biologists have suggested that the only way to recover the species is to take irrigation water away from farmers and drinking water away from the cities to ensure in-stream flows. And now, with the specter of climate change and further water scarcity hovering above the state, there are ever-more-fervent calls to retire irrigated farmlands in order to save this fish.

But defenders of the traditional acequia ecosystem and traditional chile farming as a livelihood feel that such calls are unwarranted. Paula Garcia, director of the New Mexico Acequia Association, suggests that proposed water grabs from historic irrigation systems may do more harm than good.

"You're talking about a choking off of the acequia," Paula Garcia has testified in meeting after meeting on behalf of the association. "It would be a piecemeal dismantling of this system, which [is one that] requires collective and cooperative labor."

Ironically, some of the conservation biologists with the most field experience observing the silvery minnow suggest that there are means to save the minnow in traditional acequia systems without driving the traditional cultivation of heirloom chiles and other native crops into decline.

And new research suggests that perhaps acequias aren't in direct competition with the fish for the water. In 2009, New Mexico State University published the results of a seven-year study that "validates" what four hundred years of tradition have made self-evident to the members of the New Mexico and Colorado acequias: namely, that there are huge benefits to the Rio Grande watershed through the use of acequias. During passage through an acequia, only 7 percent of the water is lost through evapotranspiration—either directly through evaporation during transit in the canals, or via water vapor released by plants during transpiration. More than 93 percent of the water is eventually returned to the system—60 percent as surface irrigation tailwater, and 33 percent as groundwater. The groundwater persists for periods of up to three months, serving as a storage bank for the river—receiving water during times of plenty and slowly releasing water back to the river during times of scarcity. Although many modern irrigation systems may no longer work like an acequia, it is nice to know that some four-hundred-year-old communal institutions still look out for the greater good.

David Cowley, an expert on fisheries and wildlife policy at New Mexico State University, has proposed the construction of what he calls propagaria in irrigation systems downstream from diversion dams on the Rio Grande, to work in consort with natural refugia for silvery minnows upstream from the dams. These constructed propagation grounds may at first seem no more than short-term Band-Aid solutions to keeping an endangered fish alive within an agricultural valley where water is becoming ever scarcer, but they are consistent with the principles of reconciliation ecology, which focuses on meeting the life history needs of endangered species in a world that is increasingly farmed and water-engineered, if not urbanized as well. The strategy of reconciliation ecology is to avoid pitting fish against farmer and urban resident from the get-go, and to use the most detailed studies of the critical needs of each endangered species to design modified environments that give them room to breathe, eat, nest, and reproduce.

If those needs can be met using the strategies proposed by David Cowley and his colleagues, perhaps the silvery minnow will not join the fifteen native species that have already been extirpated between the Rio Grande headwaters and Elephant Butte Lake. Their survival, in fact, may depend upon the chile-growing stewards of acequias along the Rio Grande, for their unlined ditches even out the subsurface flow of water from season to season, replenishing the river and its tributary streams even when drought is affecting other areas. It may seem odd that the use of water for irrigation by small-scale farmers could serve as a buffer against climate change and extinction, but studies of historic fish and bird distributions along the Upper Rio Grande support that tentative conclusion. Wherever small farms of native crops like chiles remain in a patchwork with riparian gallery forests, marshlands, and wild-running streams, there seems to be more resilience and heterogeneity in the watershed, which aids rarer species. Valuing native New Mexican chiles as part of our collective cultural heritage may be just as important as protecting the silvery minnow as part of our natural heritage, for they are two sides of the same coin.

The fire in the fireplace at Bishop's Lodge was down to a few glowing coals; the snowstorm had hit and the roads were being closed. As someone opened the closest door to the outside, a flurry of snow and a blast of chilling temperatures hit us. We decided we needed to warm up. And so we did it the New Mexico way: ordering bowls of green chile stew, red posole, and some stacked enchiladas, as well as glasses of New Mexican wine. We watched the storm roar outside the lodge's windows, humbly admitting to ourselves that the blizzard was bigger and stronger than we were.

At the same time, human activities do indeed affect the severity of weather and the impacts it has upon us. As Anna Lappé reminds us, climate change can be generated in part by what we put on the ends of our forks. In this case, we chose to reduce our carbon footprint by eating what was locally produced and minimally processed. And although the entire solution to climate change won't come simply by choosing what we put on our plates, those choices can remind us in tangible ways that reducing our "foodprint" doesn't necessarily have to leave a bad taste in our mouths.

# Chimayó Chile-Lime Butter

When Gary sent the first packet of Chimayó chiles up to Iowa some time ago, one of the first things Kurt did was invent this simple, versatile compound butter. Originally created to go on the eye-poppingly good sweet corn grown in those parts, it has since found its way onto innumerable grilled items, been stuffed inside chicken breasts—even melted over popcorn.

It doesn't exactly qualify as a traditional food, but it does really show off the deep richness of the Chimayó chile. And it's made with one of those wonderful methods that, once you get it down, is open to all manner of variation.

> 5 medium Chimayó chiles
> 2 cups (1 pound) unsalted butter, softened
> Zest of 2 limes, chopped fine
> 2 tablespoons finely chopped cilantro
> Salt to taste

Cut open and seed the chiles, and place them in a saucepan with barely enough water to cover. Bring just to a boil and then remove from heat. Allow to steep for 15 minutes. Strain the liquid from the chiles and discard, and place the chiles on a clean cutting board. Using the dull edge of a paring knife, gently scrape the soft flesh of the chile from the skin. Discard the skin, and quickly chop the flesh into a paste.

In a large mixer, beat the butter until light and smooth. Add the chile paste, lime zest, and cilantro; incorporate fully. Taste and adjust for salt.

Lay a large piece of plastic wrap out flat and smooth on a clean surface. Use a spatula to transfer the compound butter from the mixing bowl onto the plastic wrap. Carefully wrap one edge of the plastic over the butter toward the other edge, then, using your hands, shape the butter into a tube about 2 inches in diameter. Twist the two ends tight and continue to shape. Wrap this tube in foil and refrigerate or freeze. Once firm, it is ready to use, a slice at a time, for whatever your imagination suggests. Well wrapped, it will last in the refrigerator for weeks or in the freezer for months. *Yields about 2 cups, or 32 tablespoons.*

# Posole

It is a beautiful drive up into the high mesas from Albuquerque, through Santa Fe, and onward to Chimayó, where pilgrims have come for centuries to visit the shrine of Santuario de Nuestro Señor de Esquipulas. We were there on a different sort of pilgrimage, though. Immediately adjacent to the historic shrine is Léona's Restaurante de Chimayó. A shrine in its own right, Léona's is famous for tamales, but it got its start serving posole to pilgrims.

Posole is a simple stew that takes its name from the nixtamalized corn that is its main ingredient. Normally we encourage people to cook everything from scratch, but proper nixtamalization is a very tedious process that few home cooks are willing to take the time for. Commonly referred to as hominy, the nixtamal in posole is field corn that has been treated with lime (the mineral, not the fruit). This process is thought to mimic the results of the Anasazi custom of storing maize in limestone caves. Lime not only is an excellent preservative but also has many health benefits, such as improving the body's absorption of the niacin found in corn, as well as adding minerals from the lime itself, including calcium, iron, copper, and zinc.

The real reason to eat it, though, is that it tastes so marvelous. Even those of us with nary a drop of Latin blood feel the instantaneous home comfort of a steaming bowl of this rich, fragrant stew. Throughout the American Southwest and Mexico, posole is traditional for Christmas, but it's so good that you really should not limit it to once a year.

What's the secret to a good posole? As you might imagine, it's in the chiles. Real Chimayó peppers are the key. If you are not fortunate enough to live nearby, you can order them from Léona herself, strung in decorative *ristras*, at www.leonasrestaurante.com.

6 dried Chimayó chiles (or to taste)

5 pounds boned pork roast, diced into 1-inch pieces (or roast the pork whole
   and then shred it)

¼ cup olive oil or bacon fat

1 large yellow onion, diced

3 cloves garlic, sliced paper-thin

2 tablespoons dried Mexican oregano

Two 12-ounce cans whole hominy, drained and rinsed

Salt to taste

Cut open and seed the chiles, and place them in a saucepan with barely enough water to cover. Bring just to a boil and then remove from heat. Allow to steep for 15 minutes.

Meanwhile brown the pork, a little at a time, in a large stockpot with the olive oil or bacon fat, removing the browned pork to a plate. When it is all browned, sauté the onion, garlic, and oregano in the remaining fat. Add the pork back into the pot, along with enough water to cover by an inch or so. Place over high heat and bring to a boil. Reduce to a simmer and cook for 30 minutes.

While waiting for the soup to boil, strain the liquid from the chiles into the soup, and place the chiles on a clean cutting board. Using the dull edge of a paring knife, gently scrape the soft flesh of the chile from the skin. Discard the skin, and add the chile paste to the stew along with the hominy.

When the pork is tender, the soup is done. Season to taste with salt and serve. Traditional garnishes include chopped cabbage, sliced radishes, chopped onion, lime wedges, and warm corn tortillas. *Serves 6-8.*

# CHAPTER SIX

# A Peek at Our Pick of Imperiled Peppers

**AS WE LEARNED** in nursery school, or on the playgrounds of our youth, Peter Piper once picked a peck of pickled peppers. If Peter picked his peck of peppers presently, plenty of the pepper plants present in that peck would be precariously imperiled. It's not simply that the pressures posed by accelerated climate change *may* put them at risk, but that a whole slew of other factors are already affecting them: shifts in the American food distribution system; industrialization and the ever-greater dependency of our food system on long-haul trucking; the loss of farmland; the loss of specialized markets and direct markets for farmers; new pests and diseases to contend with; the demise of certain regional and ethnic food traditions; the promotion of hybrid seeds; and now the potential threat of genetically modified organisms. The list of both real and potential threats is seemingly without end.

So on a limited fuel budget, and with a lot of chile peppers to investigate, where was our Spice Ship to go? What are gastronauts to do? We simply did not have the means to visit farmers growing *all* of the imperiled peppers of North America in the same growing season, mainly because the Spice Ship had no gear that would allow for being in two places at once. (Lord knows, the three of us tried to shift into that gear once or twice during harvest time, but the loud grinding noise from the transmission gave us pause.)

What we did, instead, was use the old Pepper Parachute to air-drop one of us into a couple of other chile-growing hot spots for some all-too-brief bivouacs, just so we could at least see what else was out there in the extensive terrain we were attempting to cover. What that experience gave us were some mini sketches of the status of certain types of peppers that, in their own way, are every bit as interesting as chiltepines, habaneros, datils, Chimayós, and tabascos, albeit a bit more elusive.

Kraig was the first among us to parachute down into the farmlands of Maryland to search for a chile that is both elusive and enticing, one that a legendary seed saver named "Radish Bruce" once called "a beautiful plant and a great pepper. Its variegated leaves would look fabulous anywhere . . ."

Kraig was investigating the fish pepper, which has one of the most colorful, mysterious, apocryphal, and disputed origins of all the peppers we profiled. It's wrapped into the history of slavery in the area, and the boom and bust of the fishing industry in the Chesapeake Bay, and in fact it is thought that the decline of the fish pepper mirrors the degradation and befouling of this great bay itself. All of this, and in addition it is probably the most striking pepper plant you will ever see, with green-and-white variegated leaves, and fruit that feature "racing" stripes running down the length. The current version of its origin story states that the fish pepper hails from antebellum Maryland, an African American heirloom crop that was used in oyster and crab shacks in the area. With the fall of the oystermen and skipjack captains and of African-American-owned crab-picking houses in the region, the associated culinary use of the fish pepper has been lost and forgotten.

Kraig had the good fortune of catching up with Michael Twitty, a culinary historian and community scholar of "Afro foodways" during the slavery era in the South. By any standards, Michael is an impressive figure and memorable storyteller. He was chosen to curate the African American Heritage Seed Collection for the D. Landreth Seed Company of New Freedom, Pennsylvania. That's no small honor, since Landreth is the longest continuously operated vegetable seed house in North America; it's also the fifth-oldest corporation in the United States, so it knows what's good for business. Since 1784, Landreth has featured myriad heirlooms like the fish pepper, which Michael regards as being among the true prizes in Landreth's "hall of fame" for vegetable seeds rooted in African American cultures.

Michael began to tell Kraig his interpretation of the origins of the fish pepper: "I think there is an alternate explanation to the fish pepper's history. You see, seed catalogs only go back until the 1870s. The slave trade in Maryland stopped in the mid-1700s. But there were a lot of folks being smuggled in as well as free blacks coming from West Africa and the Caribbean—predominantly they came from Sene-gambia, Angola, and Ghana, but also a number from Barbados, Jamaica, and Santo Domingo."

And yet, while the fish pepper probably came to the United States via the Caribbean—the way station for transits to the East Coast from Africa—the details of its origins remain difficult to pin down, since most African American communities at that time had oral rather than written histories. The Swedish naturalist Peter Kalm noted that forms of "guinea peppers" were grown and eaten among black slaves as early as 1748, but it is odd that no naturalists or garden journalists specifically mention the variegated foliage of fish pepper, which sets them apart from nearly all other heirloom chiles.

What's more, Thomas Jefferson's observations on vegetables, flowers, and fruits in Washington, DC–area markets refer more to ornamental than to culinary uses of peppers. Peter Hatch, an agricultural historian who is director of gardens and grounds at Monticello, has documented cayenne peppers growing in Jefferson's own gardens as early as 1767, but there's no mention of the fish pepper, either in Jefferson's own food production plots or in those of the slaves from whom he regularly purchased vegetables. Perhaps the fish pepper was at first considered by whites of that era as a plant suitable only for "show," while African American slaves and freemen had already begun to use these ornamentals in their own foods. It is speculated that the flashy lime-green-and-white foliage of fish pepper may be the result of a chance chromosomal mutation (a "sport," in horticultural jargon) of a more common green-leaved serrano pepper prior to the 1880s, but there is no real means of verifying the time and place of such a mutation after the fact.

The particular presence of fish pepper pods and their two-tone foliage wasn't noted in print until 1901. That's when Harry Franklyn Hall, the famed chef of Boothby's Hotel in Philadelphia, made mention of them in his rambling recipe book, *300 Ways to Cook and Serve Shell Fish, Terrapin, and Green Turtle*. Hall observed that this pepper was sold in fish markets in the mid-Atlantic alongside terrapin, shellfish, and fish, for it was often used in sauces for these seafoods. One of those sauces was called *piccalilli* when a recipe for it was included in B. C. Howard's 1881 classic, *Fifty Years in a Maryland Kitchen*. However, Michael Twitty has suggested that the name *piccalilli* wrongly links fish pepper sauces to British culinary traditions rather than to African American traditions. His suggestion to Kraig was that, if one looked a little deeper, a linguistic linkage could be made to a name for peppers that is now widespread in Africa and the Caribbean: *pilipili*.

*Pilipili,* it turns out, is the name for red peppers in Swahili, Zulu, and Lingala dialects from sub-Saharan Africa, but it is entomologically related to *berbere, fulful,* and *filfil*. Those terms were first used for black pepper in North Africa and the Middle East, and later applied to red peppers or chiles. As Kraig learned, the original name for the pungent fish sauce made with peppers on the edge of the Chesapeake Bay may have been a variant of the ancient term *pilipili*. By Michael Twitty's reckoning, that name might have arrived in Maryland with West African slaves or, more likely, with their descendants from the Caribbean—both regions where many kinds of peppers had long been grown.

The slaves brought up from the Caribbean could have also carried along in their heads a recipe for a spicy fish, pork, or chicken dish historically called pepper pot. Kraig did some sleuthing and found that pepper pot is still occasionally prepared in the metro Philadelphia area just to the north of rural Maryland, and it is also the subject of a famous 1811 John Lewis Krimmel painting called *Pepper-Pot: A Scene in the Philadelphia Market*, in which a barefoot black woman is ladling out soup to white customers. Pepper pot is still served in the Caribbean, made with the locally available meats of chicken and pork. These dishes seem to be a derivative of the West African dish known as *callaloo*, a spicy vegetable stew. All this speculation has somehow reinforced the notion that such piquant sauces, soups, and meat dishes were derived from English cuisine—a notion that Michael Twitty finds a bit ridiculous, since Anglo-Americans at that time had little exposure to or tolerance for pungent foods compared with African slaves who had survived the diaspora.

That being said, we do know that in the late nineteenth and early twentieth centuries, fish peppers were featured in fish sauces from Philadelphia, Baltimore, and Washington, DC, and that they came largely from the dooryard gardens of African American cooks, waiters, and dishwashers who worked in crab shacks, oyster houses, and fish market cafés. Garden historian Jack Staub has noted that, around Baltimore, the reputation of fish peppers once reached almost mythic status:

> There was a local African American legend which held that in order for peppers to achieve their ultimate fieriness, [their grower] had to be in a fiery state as well. Therefore, the best fish peppers were said to be planted by those who were really angry . . .

Before the mid-twentieth century, when the Chesapeake Bay suffered massive environmental degradation, the fish pepper and the seafood that it accompanied were in their heyday. The pepper would be picked fresh and finely chopped to accompany a wide range of comestible critters, from blue crabs and flounder to diamondback terrapin and green sea turtles. As its pods turned fire-engine red and dried in the sun, they would be crushed and incorporated into a wide variety of oyster sauces, fish soups, clam chowders, and everything-but-the-kitchen-sink bouillabaisses. But by the 1950s, polluted runoff into the bay and shellfish diseases began to decimate the bounty that had once been taken for granted. In turn, the authentic bayside crab shacks and oyster houses went into decline, and their business was taken over by second-rate versions well within the safe and sanitized confines of the cities. By the 1980s, when two more diseases ravaged the oysters of the Chesapeake, most of Maryland's historic oyster houses had gone down for the count, and with them had vanished the culture that had nurtured the fish pepper.

In the course of his visit, Kraig got the impression that African American gardeners and farmers who are still growing the fish pepper are few and far between. Michael Twitty himself is one. Greg Thorne of Westminster, Maryland, now grows fish peppers among the produce from the four-and-a-half-acre farm that he and his wife, Kris, take to local farmer's markets, but Greg was quick to admit to Kraig that it is not really a part of his family's tradition. His grandfather was an African American farmer who passed on the traditions of growing okra, yams, crowder peas, and beans to Greg's father, but Greg doesn't remember his father growing much in the way of peppers, and certainly not the fish pepper.

"I'd like to tell you that we've been cultivating this pepper for years," Kris told Kraig, "and that his father [pointing to Greg] and his grandfather planted it. But really, we found it in the catalog and thought it sounded interesting. We really don't know anyone else who grows this, nor who has used it in dishes. It is a really beautiful pepper, though . . ."

Michael Twitty thinks he knows why the fish pepper has not, until recently, been on many African Americans' screens as an element of their cultural heritage: "We were an agrarian people for millennia—even through the period of slavery—but we went from being 90 percent agrarian to 90 percent urban in less than a hundred years . . . think about that!"

Nevertheless, Greg and Kris Thorne now see interest in the fish pepper growing among other nearby market gardeners, and among

# Domestication of the Chile Pepper: So Good, It Happened Five Times

The term *chile pepper* actually describes any fruit of the plants belonging to the genus *Capsicum,* comprising twenty-two species, all of which can be found in the Western Hemisphere. While this term is principally used in the United States to describe the fruits of the species *C. annuum*–including bell peppers, jalapeños, serranos, and Anaheims–there are other domesticated species in the genus that deserve our attention as well: *C. chinense* (habanero, Scotch bonnets), *C. frutescens* (tabasco), *C. baccatum* (ají), and *C. pubescens* (chile manzano). *Capsicum* is the only member of the Solanaceae, or nightshade, family that uses the pungency of capsaicin instead of toxic alkaloids to manage pests and seed-spoiling microbes. Most other nightshades– belladonna, tobacco, tomatoes, potatoes, eggplants, and jimsonweed–rely on an altogether different set of chemical defenses.

Although chile peppers share their geographic and evolutionary origins with such important foods as the tomato and potato, they have another historical distinction: Chile peppers are one of the few crops to have been domesticated more than once and in different locations. There are, of course, a few other crops in the "polyphyletic" set. Cotton, wheat, and New World beans (lima, runner, pinto, tepary, and green beans) were domesticated in multiple regions: cotton in Mexico, South America, Africa, and Asia; wheat in Turkey and the southern Levant; and beans in both Mexico and the western reaches of South America. But various *Capsicums* were domesticated both in Mexico (*C. annuum, C. pubescens,*

---

chefs as well. Their neighbor and fellow vendor at the Downtown Westminster Farmer's Market, Jackie Coldsmith, now grows a few fish peppers at De La Tierra Gardens in nearby Taneytown. And down along the bay in northern Virginia, Lawrence and Becky Latané have put in twenty to thirty fish pepper plants at Blenheim Organic Gardens, immediately south of George Washington's Birthplace National Monument. The Latané family has cultivated that ground for more than fifty years, with Lawrence taking over the tractor seat for the last nine, after leaving his job as a staff writer for the *Richmond Times-Dispatch*. Kraig found that Lawrence's fish pepper plants don't reach the size of the other heirloom chile varieties he grows for the farmer's market in Colonial and *C. frutescens*) and in South America (*C. chinense, C. baccatum*). This means that on separate occasions, on separate continents, early humans were interested enough in wild pepper species to harvest, use, and plant them, selecting individual plants that had desirable traits. Yet whereas cotton provides a great fiber and cloth for many uses, and wheat and beans are staple foods, chile peppers are not essential to the food security and nutritional health of a nascent agricultural society. So, obviously, the appeal of chile peppers goes well beyond their nutritional value.

### Wild to Tame?

Most wild peppers have small, upright fruits, which when ripe fall right off the plant upon the slightest touch–facilitating the dispersion of seeds by birds. With minor exceptions, these wild fruits tend to be exceedingly *hot*. Much like the domestication of dogs, during which humans eliminated aggression and other anti-human behaviors, the chiles that were culturally selected became larger, with more variety in color, shape, and size; for the most part, too, their heat levels became more tame. That's because attracting human stewards became another evolutionary strategy for chiles, ensuring their protection, cultivation, and subsequent reproduction, so that their pungency need not be their only means of defense.

By the 1500s, the early Spanish conquistadores recorded that the Aztecs had named dozens of distinctive varieties in their Nahuatl language, all with different shapes, colors, and culinary uses. Today, five hundred years later, the domestication process is still enriching the diversity of chile varieties, as Latin American farmers recruit and select other forms from the wild and hybridize already domesticated selections to create novel forms.

Kraig

Williamsburg, but they are sweeter and have a level of heat quite different from the others—perhaps not as hot as advertised.

Between the efforts made by Michael, Greg, Jackie, and Lawrence over the last few years, Kraig provisionally tallied far less than two hundred fish pepper plants that are being grown in their region of origin. That's not a lot. So few, in fact, that Slow Food has included the pepper on its International Ark of Taste, and Gary has listed it as endangered on the Renewing America's Food Traditions checklist of foods at risk in North America.

It isn't simply the fish pepper that has been losing ground among the once vast arable lands surrounding the Chesapeake in Maryland,

Virginia, and out to southeastern Pennsylvania. These states have been rapidly losing their agricultural lands, whether fish peppers are grown on them or not. Over the last fifty years, Virginia has lost five million acres of its farmland to development, so that today less than two-thirds of the land cultivated or grazed in 1960 remains in production. Maryland has lost more than a million and a half acres of farmland over the same period.

If those trends don't make it tough enough for a farmer to survive, consider the predictions that global warming will further shrink the landmass surrounding Chesapeake Bay that will remain above sea level. Scientists have calculated that, over the last century, the Chesapeake's water levels have likely risen almost a foot. The scientists suggest that this rise in water levels is not only due to sea level rises triggered by ice caps melting and global warming, but also due to land subsidence and shifts in flood discharges resulting from the rapid suburbanization of former farmlands. But if current predictions of global sea level rises for the next century are at all accurate, the water level in the bay is likely to rise at least twice as much this century as it did during the last hundred years. The spread of the bay's waters into some former coastal farmlands is likely to occur as a result of local acceleration of land subsidence, since sedimentation rates have been forever changed by the manipulation of the watersheds above the bay.

Nonetheless, if it seems as though the fish pepper has reached its last straw, look again, this time at One Straw Farm near Whitehall, Maryland. That's where fiery food fanatic Mick T. Kipp transplanted out his first thirty fish pepper plants, and where he hopes their production will expand like a pirate's empire out at sea. Mick not only dresses like a pirate on occasion but also runs the Whiskey Island Pirate Shop in Baltimore, which serves a sizzlin' Sunday brunch. He's a former stuntman who became a chef and natural foods marketer after a bout of cancer, and who now generously supports cancer centers with his earnings from fish peppers and other spices. In fact, he calls himself the "Maker and Purveyor of All-Natural, Small-Batch, Hand-Made Spice Blends and Specialty Foods" that carry wild names like Ras el

Pyrate, Swamp Pop, and the Juke Joint Mojo Pulled Pork Barbecue Sandwich.

Needless to say, the guy has an imagination and, in this case, a good deal of vision for someone who hangs out with lots of other pirates prone to wearing eye patches. Part of his current vision is focused on the fish pepper, for he is aspiring to "re-integrate the endangered African-American heirloom pepper of the Chesapeake 'Crab Cake' foodshed back to prominence in our local cuisine!"

After following Mick's high-profile promotions for the last year, the gastronauts reached a quick consensus: If it takes a pirate to release further pressure on an imperiled pepper, Mick is the right pirate for the job.

At about the same time as Kraig's trip to the Chesapeake, Gary parachuted into the field, but far away from the ocean with its pirates and fish peppers. He landed not far from where he grew up, in the Indiana Dunes on Lake Michigan's shores, and even closer to where he first worked on a farm that almost straddled the Illinois–Wisconsin border.

The threatened heirloom for which he fell out of the sky is called the Beaver Dam pepper. Unlike other peppers that we visited together, this one involves not some ancient link between a particular people and a place, but a much more fluid relationship between more recent immigrants to America and an heirloom they brought with them from eastern Europe, and then adapted to their adopted homeland. The Beaver Dam pepper first took root in American soil among Hungarian, Austrian, and German immigrants to the Upper Midwest, but it has remained mobile, following the descendants of its first stewards to other places as well.

Gary first encountered Beaver Dam in the grow-out gardens of the Seed Savers Exchange, in Decorah, Iowa, when he served on that organization's board. It was a thick-fleshed, rather meaty pepper relative to the more famous paprikas of eastern Europe, and so defied easy stereotyping. When he encountered it again in the nurseries and on the seed racks of Jung Seeds—a distinguished regional seed house based in southern Wisconsin—he knew he had to learn more of its story. One of the Jung's extended family informed him that the family that first championed this heirloom chile could still be found around Beaver Dam, Wisconsin, not all that far from Jung's own grow-out farm. Gary eventually worked up the nerve to make a cold call to one of the remaining family residences in the town of Beaver Dam, where David and MaryAnn Hussli were reported to live.

MaryAnn fielded the call and confirmed that her husband, David, was indeed the grandson of Joseph Hussli Senior, the man who introduced and adapted pepper seeds brought from Hungary to the Beaver Dam vicinity. But then she threw Gary a curveball—he needn't parachute into their town of Beaver Dam, because the family's pepper seeds weren't really there in the family anymore! They had gone south with David's brother Larry, who remained the keeper of their family seed stock, but at his home down in Edwardsville, Illinois, not far from St. Louis.

That was good news for Gary, whose in-laws live within the St. Louis metro area, and whose favorite cultural landscape in the entire Midwest is the Cahokia Mounds that rise high above the Mississippi River floodplain between Edwardsville and St. Louis.

Gary called upon Larry one Saturday morning and found that he was not only willing to talk, but excited to correct some earlier versions of Beaver Dam pepper history that were fraught with errors: "You see, I was born and raised with that pepper, and I usually try to grow 350 to 500 plants of it. I do it nearly every year."

While Larry has been keeping Beaver Dam peppers in his garden for roughly forty years, he said he was simply following in his father's footsteps. And his father, Joseph John Hussli, took up the torch from his own father in Beaver Dam, Joe Hussli the Elder, an immigrant from Hungary who unfortunately died before Larry could learn directly from him. Larry's father and mother were among several Hungarian immigrant families that grew the heirloom pepper in Dodge County, Wisconsin, when he was growing up, but all of them traced their seeds and knowledge back to what Joe the Elder brought over from the Old

World: "The seeds raised by several Hungarian families around Beaver Dam all came from my granddad's seeds. But my dad also had a passion for them. He regularly grew twenty-five hundred pepper plants a season, and sold the peppers locally."

Larry has done his own sleuthing about his family's origin and immigration through websites for Ellis Island and other ports of entry, as well as through chat groups of Hungarian Americans. He has verified that his grandfather came over (presumably with the pepper seeds tucked away in his garments) from Apatin, Hungary, around 1912. But the Hussli home just prior to emigration was near the Hungary–Austria border, in a region where many of the residents had German ancestry. Their German roots were not something they felt comfortable claiming as they tried to gain US citizenship; many concealed that fact when they arrived in America after the world wars.

"From what I can trace, the Hussli family in Apatin goes back to the mid-1700s," Larry noted, though he's not as sure about the length of tenure of the Beaver Dam pepper on Hungarian soil. Nevertheless, he's gotten in touch with other Hungarian Americans from the same area, and he's made a gift of the Beaver Dam pepper seeds to more than one hundred people descended from that area who now live in the United States, Canada, and other parts of the world. Regardless of the antiquity of this link between their ancestors and this seed stock, many of the recipients of Beaver Dam seeds know this crop as part of their shared heritage.

Gary asked Larry about what he thought were the optimal growing conditions for this plant, since it had shifted its geography at least three times: once from the New World to the Old; then from Austria back to the Americas, when the Husslis settled in Wisconsin; and, more recently, when Larry moved from Beaver Dam—in the climatic belt buffered by the presence of Lake Michigan nearby—to the flood-fertilized valleys of southern Illinois.

Larry pointed out that the Hussli family has actually selected two distinct peppers out of the original gene pool, adapting them to the climate and growing conditions of the Midwest: The true Beaver

Dam heirloom has longer, pointier pods. The related tomato pepper is shorter, rounder, and actually shaped like some tomatoes. He says that both Beaver Dam and the tomato pepper are much more thick-fleshed than any Hungarian paprikas he's seen, so he wouldn't bet that they're from the very same "bloodline."

He reminded Gary that not all peppers in eastern Europe are necessarily dried and ground into paprika powder. Eastern and southern Europeans love stuffing peppers and tomatoes, just as they did with eggplants and calabashes, before these other vegetables were introduced. Because Beaver Dam peppers are fleshy, they don't immediately dry as well as paprika types, but that doesn't mean that they have limited usefulness. Like many backyard plant breeders, Larry has continued to evaluate and select his family heirlooms with the goal of improving their culinary qualities, rather than keeping them static.

"They can give you plenty of flavor, not just fire. My favorite way of eating them is raw, cut in half and then into slices [but *not* in rings, as some claim his mother Florence once told them], and then paired with some venison sausage I make and some cheddar cheese." He also eats them fresh, stuffed with a spreadable cheese, and has paired them with many meats, including salami and liver sausage, and Swiss and other cheeses.

Although he's renting a piece of land near his Edwardsville home, a couple of hundred miles south of where his grandfather and father grew the pepper, Larry feels that "the temperature is better for it down here—longer growing seasons. I usually have a great crop, but, like any farming situation, you're always at the mercy of the weather." So as a buffer from the climatic vagaries, he starts some of his Beaver Dam and tomato pepper seeds in two of his own little greenhouses, and he gives an equal amount of seeds to a friend with a commercial greenhouse nearby to have some backup crop as insurance.

"I've been raising them for approximately forty years, and the one thing I've learned is that there is no need to rush them, to get them in too early. Where I live now, I get them in the ground two weeks earlier than I could in Beaver Dam up north anyway."

There is a certain irony in the fact that Larry has taken the Beaver Dam peppers to a hotter, more southerly climate. Since the time when he grew up around his father's pepper patch, the climate of southern Wisconsin has become far more like that of southern Illinois. Mean annual temperatures in Wisconsin rose 1.3° F from 1950 to 2006, with winter temperatures warming by 2.5° F over that same period. The Union of Concerned Scientists has projected that, by 2030, Wisconsin summers may resemble those of Illinois in terms of average temperature and rainfall. By century's end, UCS scientists predict, Wisconsin's summer climate will generally resemble that of present-day Arkansas and Missouri—not far from the conditions under which Larry Hussli is already growing Beaver Dam peppers.

If Larry's selection of his family heirlooms has helped to better adapt Beaver Dam peppers to the current climate around Edwardsville and St. Louis, he would do his former neighbors in Wisconsin a big favor by sending some of his seed northward once more. The Husslis would then become involved in an adaptation process that certain ecologists term *assisted migration,* one that moves genetic resources to climates more like those they historically experienced, in order to prepare them for future changes.

Gary had one last question for Larry Hussli before they said goodbye. He wanted to know what his fundamental motivation was for keeping his family's heirloom vegetable in circulation, and out of reach of the dark hand of extinction. "Why do you do it? Why do you go to this effort year after year to keep the rare Beaver Dam pepper alive and thriving?"

Larry was quick to answer, for the Beaver Dam pepper has been part of his own seasonal cycle for upward of forty years. That's given him some time to think such questions through.

"All I wanna do is honor my grandfather and father. Some of the rest of my family doesn't garden, but I do, and so I can keep it alive. I just like to promote this pepper and spread the seeds around, I don't care about any laurels or income out of it for myself. But I do like to eat them . . . I bet that I average putting up fifty to sixty pints of peppers per year. That

# Don't Count on Genetic Engineering to Save Food Production from Climate Change

In the February 12, 2010 edition of the journal *Science,* a panel of food industry scientists proposed that "radical new directions will be needed in food production to deal with climate change," including genetic engineering of food crops. The panel, convened by Secretary of State Hillary Clinton's science and technology adviser Nina Federoff, urged world leaders "to get beyond popular biases against agricultural biotechnology," claiming that transgenic crops can most effectively produce greater yields under harsher conditions such as droughts, hot summers, and saline soils.

But such a claim is no radically new direction. Over the last several years, some of the biggest corporations in the world have been out to grab every "climate-ready" patent for food crops that they can get. Just three multinational corporations—DuPont, BASF, and Monsanto—account for two-thirds of the patents for "climate-ready" GMO technologies that have been proposed or already issued. At the time of this writing, six large corporations and two of their biotech partners appear to control 77 percent of all climate-ready crop plant patents. Some of the work toward these patents has been going on for well over a decade, but will they ever achieve the goals that the corporations claim for them? Let's look at what some of the most respected crop breeders and plant biologists say about this.

In 2004, the Commission for Environmental Cooperation of North America asked some of the most esteemed scientists in the world–including maize breeder Major Goodman, plant conservationist Peter Raven, sustainable agriculture expert David Andow, and genetic resource expert Garrison Wilkes–to evaluate such claims, particularly for GMO corn. Here is their response to the claim that transgenic biotechnologies are the best way to gain the needed drought tolerance for corn to adapt to a drier, warmer world:

gives me more than enough to tide me over through the winter, so that I can eat them just about every day of the year if I want to."

At the same time that Larry is engaged in conservation of heirloom peppers and preservation of related culinary traditions, he also makes room for innovations that keep this pepper legacy dynamic. He has—by his own hand—hybridized the Beaver Dam with the tomato pepper and is now selecting a third variety.

"I did the cross with a little brush, and from those seeds, I've gotten

Drought tolerance might potentially be greatly affected by a single gene [suitable for transfer to a crop], but the evidence for this is slim, and the single gene certainly has not been publicly identified. The obvious answer is that cactus and maize differ by more than a few genes, and probably none of them [that is, none of the genes, when transferred from one plant to the other] would enable widespread cultivation of maize across the Sahara or Atacama . . . [In short], plant breeding is unlikely to be radically altered by genetic engineering, despite progress in genomics. New traits will ultimately be added to today's breeding goals, but most are likely to require several decades of development.

Such biotechnological research and development is likely to cost ten to fifty times more per crop variety than conventional plant breeding, and thousands of times more than careful evaluation of existing food crop diversity for its immediately useful adaptations to drought and other harsh conditions. Although there is already at least one transgenic chile pepper that has been tested in experimental plots, it has not yet been commercially released. It is not clear at all that such new releases will be adopted by farmers, nor whether they have any concrete advantages in changing climatic regimes over the many chile pepper varieties already accessible to farmers.

One thing, however, is for sure: The second "Green Revolution" proposed by Clinton's science adviser and her corporate allies is likely to be the costliest invest-ment—economically, and perhaps ecologi-cally as well—of any plant-breeding initiative in the history of humankind. Whether it will produce yield results commensurate to the claims remains to be seen. Prudence suggests that a vast array of other agricul-tural strategies may be far more cost-effec-tive in sustaining chile pepper yields over the long haul than reliance on the "silver bullet" biotechnologies being proposed by industry.

Gary

a somewhat different pepper that's bigger and thicker and crunchier. I hope my dad and granddad won't think bad of me for messing around a little with their originals . . . but I keep the originals, too; they're just something I don't ever want to be lost."

Of course, many peppers are being lost to American farms, gardens, and tables as we write this. The Seed Savers Exchange has documented that more than two hundred varieties of sweet and hot peppers have disappeared from the seed trade in North America since 1981. Some had names that hinted at their origins, like Czechoslovakian Black Sweet, Hungarian Rainbow Wax Short, Mild California, Missouri Wonder, Ozark Giant, Rio Grande 66, Romanian White Gypsy Sweet, Tennessee Firecracker, Texas, Wisconsin Lakes, and Wild Grove. If they have survived somewhere, undocumented, would they still be able to grow in their original areas of origin? Has climate change begun to rupture the time-tested connections between pepper and place?

Kurt's solo recon mission took him to a place not normally regarded as a chile pepper hot spot, but known instead as the Nutmeg State—Connecticut. But the story actually started in southern Italy, in the mountainous region of Basilicata—what one might call the "instep of the boot." Basilicata's two subregions, Potenza and Matera, have small coastlines on the Tyrrhenian and Ionian Seas, respectively. And in central Potenza, due east of Naples, sits the tiny town of Ruoti.

For several years there, Giuseppe Nardiello and his wife, Angela, nurtured a favorite variety of sweet frying pepper. When they set sail from the port of Naples in 1887 for a new life beside the Golden Door, Angela carried her one-year-old daughter Anna and a handful of the pepper seeds with them. They settled in Naugatuck, Connecticut, where they raised the peppers, and eleven children. The fourth one was a son named Jimmy.

Jimmy's son James, who was eighty-one and still residing in Naugatuck, told Kurt that the teachers in Jimmy's grade school dropped the *i* from Nardiello, apparently believing that theirs was the proper spelling. It stuck to Jimmy, and to all the subsequent siblings and descendants.

James also said that his father was the only one of the Nardello children to inherit Angela's love of the garden, and that Jimmy lovingly cared for his own plot throughout his life. He built them the way his mother taught him, in terraces, the way all gardens were built in the mountains of southern Italy. There he grew hundreds of peppers, but the sweet frying pepper was his favorite, and he would string up his bounty and hang them to dry in the shed, so his family could enjoy them all winter long.

Jimmy passed away in 1983. But before he did, he donated some of the heirloom pepper seeds to Seed Savers Exchange. It has since become known as Jimmy Nardello's Sweet Italian Frying Pepper.

One hundred twenty years after the Nardellos set sail from Italy, bringing a small piece of their homeland with them, the pepper that bears the family name is becoming a favorite among chefs and home gardeners nationwide, and it has recently been moved to the category of "Success Stories" on Slow Food USA's Ark of Taste—an indication that its popularity is growing among home and specialty growers, and that the variety no longer needs "extraordinary efforts to keep it alive and in the hands of gardeners, farmers, and chefs," in the words of Ben Watson, co-chair of Slow Food USA's Biodiversity Committee, and himself a lifetime listed member of Seed Savers Exchange.

Each year, in gardens around the country (including Kurt's), the Nardellos turn color, from their youthful kelly green to a mature fire-engine red, indicating that they are ready to be picked, sliced, fried in olive oil with garlic, and slathered over steaks alongside a generous pour of Primitivo.

The best ones resemble a pig's ear. James says that's how his dad picked them. They grow in full sun in neutral to acidic soil, and they are quite prolific as long as they are not overwatered.

"I first grew this pepper in my own New Hampshire garden in the early 1990s," Ben Watson said, "and it is extraordinarily dependable, and always delicious—long, sweet, and with a mild, spicy flavor. About the only negative is sometimes the peppers are so long and heavy that the plants need to be staked, but that's true of several heirloom peppers I've grown."

There are, of course, peppers as rare and as delicious as the Fish, the Beaver Dam, and the Jimmy Nardello that have not yet blinked out of the all-star lineup in America. There is the Hinkelhatz hot pepper, with a pod shape that the Pennsylvania Dutch liken to a chicken heart, which is what *Hinkelhatz* means in German. Virgil Ainsworth's Rooster Spur heirloom has been grown by his family in Laurel, Mississippi, for more than a century, and it is still used in those parts to spice Rooster Pepper sausage. Wenk's Yellow Hot is an heirloom unlike other chiles from northern New Mexico; it achieved notoriety in Albuquerque's South Valley, not far from where Joseph Jaramillo grows his Isleta native chiles. Reimer Seeds in Mount Holly, North Carolina, carries the rare Tennessee Teardrops pepper, an old heirloom from the Hog and Hominy State whose thick-fleshed, tapered pods grow upright, turning from pale green to yellow with purple stripes to reddish black as they mature. Texas has its MacMahon's selection of the semi-wild Bird Pepper, Pennsylvania its Weaver's Mennonite Stuffing sweet pepper from Lancaster County, and Virginia its Doe Hill from Highland County.

These rarities give us (and our parachutes) pause, making us reflect on the great diversity of plants nurtured by the people on this continent over the centuries. The question is not simply whether we will keep the heirloom varieties of the past alive as pieces of living history. The question is whether we can keep our crops dynamically adapting to place in the face of impending climate change—no matter how severe—so that this remarkable diversity that has been passed on from our ancestors can offer food security and pleasure to our progeny.

As longtime Seed Savers Exchange board member and agricultural law expert Neil Hamilton recently wrote:

> Regardless of your view on climate change, agriculture needs to become more resilient. Perhaps our "unusually" wet fall that delayed harvests—and caused millions in crop losses in the South [with more than a billion dollars requested for farmer disaster relief in 2009]—was just "the weather." But what if it's a preview of how climate change may increase farming's vulnerability? We care about our future, so we should plan for how we may need to adapt.

Our own view, from the perspective of the Spice Ship, suggests that one fundamental strategy for gaining more resilience in our food system is to begin *rediversifying* the varieties of each crop that we grow. In other words, we shouldn't be putting all our peppers in one basket, for the uncertainty factor associated with global climate change is, and will continue to be, huge. And the more kinds of crops we eat, the higher the likelihood that our dietary needs will be met in a balanced way as well.

In the case of peppers, promoting the consumption of many varieties may bring us greater pleasure—or even a bit of fleeting pain—but never a dull moment.

# Stuffed Beaver Dam Peppers, Spanish-Style

The Beaver Dam pepper hails from Hungary by way of the eponymous town in Wisconsin, so preparing it in a Spanish style would only come to mind for a chef who owns a Spanish restaurant. In northern Spain, this dish would be prepared with the signature chile, the piquillo. When Kurt first laid regional hands on a Beaver Dam, though, he said to himself, here's a stuffing pepper that might be even better suited to the dish.

These peppers are stuffed with salt cod, which requires a little time and attention to work with. It's not difficult or complicated, but it does demand a pinch of planning.

Stuffing the peppers itself is a slightly delicate matter simply because handling the peppers or overstuffing them could lead to tearing them. No worries if you do, though; simply squeeze them back together, reclaim any excess filling, and keep going.

To make this dish with the fresh peppers, you'll need to roast them first. There are a number of ways to roast any kind of chile, but they all rely on the same principle: Char the skin, then sweat it and peel it. Using a grill or a broiler, or placing them directly on a gas burner, roast each pepper, turning occasionally until it's blistered and charred on each side. Place them in a paper bag, roll up the top to seal, and let stand for about twenty minutes. Remove them from the bag and gently scrape off the skin with a paring knife. Then simply cut off the tops and remove the seeds. Your peppers are now ready for stuffing.

1 pound salt cod
1 medium Idaho potato, peeled and boiled
½ cup extra-virgin olive oil
1 medium yellow onion, peeled and minced
3 cloves garlic, peeled and sliced paper-thin
2 tablespoons chopped fresh parsley

½ bay leaf

½ teaspoon ground nutmeg

1 cup dry white wine

2 eggs, beaten

15–20 Beaver Dam peppers, roasted, peeled, and seeded

Sauce

One 12-ounce can crushed tomatoes

½ yellow onion, minced

1 clove garlic, peeled and sliced paper-thin

½ teaspoon sweet smoked paprika (also known as pimentón)

Salt to taste

### To Reconstitute the Salt Cod

Rinse the cod thoroughly to remove any excess crystallized salt from the surface. Place the fish in a shallow glass baking dish with enough water to cover and refrigerate for 24 hours, changing the water at least three times over that course of time. Remove the fish and discard the water, then rinse a final time.

### To Make the Stuffing

Chop the fish into chunks, then shred with forks. It should be mostly boneless, but be sure to remove any you may come across. Coarsely mash the potato and add it to the fish.

In a large sauté pan, heat the oil over medium heat and add the onion. Toss briefly in the oil, then add the garlic, parsley, bay leaf, and nutmeg. Sauté a few more minutes until the onion is translucent and tender. Deglaze by adding the white wine, then return to the heat and allow to simmer for roughly 10 minutes, or until nearly all the liquid is evaporated. Remove from the heat and let stand 10 to 15 minutes to cool.

Meanwhile, make the sauce by simmering the crushed tomatoes with the onion, garlic, and paprika over medium-low heat for 15 to 20 minutes, then season to taste with salt.

Preheat the oven to 400°F.

Combine the onion mixture with the cod and potatoes, then fold in the beaten eggs. Mix thoroughly and gently spoon the filling into each of the roasted peppers. Use a small spoon to help avoid tearing the peppers. Arrange in a baking dish that just fits all the peppers (9 x 9 is a good bet) and cover with the sauce. Bake for about 20 minutes or until bubbly.

Serve immediately, garnished with your favorite shredded cheese. *Serves 4 as an entrée or 8 as an appetizer.*

# Eating and Growing Food in Ways That Counter Climate Change

**AS THE THREE** of us traveled the continent in our Spice Ship for nearly a year, many of those whom we visited in various hot spots asked us just what we thought our responses to climate change should be. For both food producers and eaters, our answer may have at first seemed too simple to be of much immediate help, given the rapidity of change and degree of uncertainty we are facing:

"Eat and farm as if the earth matters, as we should have been doing all along. Regardless of how quickly we can implement the specific fixes being proposed to mitigate climate change, we all need to reduce our carbon *foodprint* and adapt to change in ways that keep the earth's bounty as diverse, as delicious, and as resilient as possible."

In essence, what we are suggesting is that good farming practices—for chiles or for any other crop—make sense both ecologically and economically and should be supported even if climate change is not roaring down upon us. Likewise, the very same ethical and ecological principles that may guide us out of the climate crisis in the long run will also make our food system more sensible, sustainable, equitable, and enjoyable every day of our lives. If the fear of climate change is the only motivation we have to encourage change in our eating habits, our food system, and our use of this earth, we doubt that most folks will be motivated to accept change. But if adapting to climate change also brings with it other blessings that can potentially enrich rather than impoverish our lives, such as better health and the pleasures of the table, more folks will come on board and participate. Of course, these issues apply only to those of us who eat.

So let's look at some guiding principles that might help us along. We've gleaned these insights from the many conversations the three of us have had together, and have had with dozens of farmers, foragers, chefs, and scientists over the last few years.

**Principle 1:** Now, more than ever before, we need a diversity of food crop varieties in our fields and orchards in order to be able to adapt to change, and to keep our food system healthy, resilient, and delicious. Explore, celebrate, and consume what diversity can be found locally.

Our interest in heirloom chile peppers is twofold: It is about redis-covering the strong links among food, culture, and identity, but it is also not so much about preserving the past as it is about investing in the future. Years ago, farmers did not plant solely chiles; they also grew some beans, maize, fruit trees, tomatoes, bell peppers, and other types of vegetables. Diversity in the field is one of our best bet-hedging strate-gies to deal with climatic instability and uncertainty: No single geneti-cally engineered seed or breed will allow us to shift in time to adapt to the changing weather, pests, and diseases farmers will be facing over the next century. By growing many varieties of one crop, and many different crops, we create a diverse portfolio; we don't know which ones will provide strong returns in our uncertain climate future, but by spreading our "investment" around we have not risked everything on one or two choices. Storing seeds in gene banks as a backup insurance plan is necessary, but not enough: Farmers need to be actively evaluating, experimenting, and improving crop plants in their agroecological habitats as those habitats shift.

The heterogeneity of plant populations and mixtures of crop varieties in the same field can reduce the impact of introduced pests and diseases as well. And this diversity can keep our food system more resilient in many other ways. Having a diversity of food crops not only keeps our agricultural lands healthy, but keeps our own bodies healthy as well. Every region in the United States has local and traditional food specialties—from cider to seafood and salad greens—all of it much better for you and for your neighbors than most "imported" food. Go out and find it. As our friend Poppy Tooker says, "You've got to eat it to save it!"

**Principle 2:** Farmers' knowledge and problem-solving skills are key assets for coping with and adapting to climate change, assets that have not yet been sufficiently honored, understood, and drawn upon by the scientific community.

Time after time during our spice odyssey, we were amazed and impressed by the insights farmers had about how they have adapted to a changing climate. They were not in denial—as the American Farm Bureau Federation's bureaucrats may well be—nor were they sitting back as passive victims, playing the blame game. Instead, many of the farmers we met were already adapting to changing ecological conditions and markets, using their individual intelligence, collective cultural wisdom, and sophisticated skills to dynamically manage their resources. They need support from consumers to continue to do so, and incentives—not barriers from their governments—for thinking outside the box.

**Principle 3:** Eaters—or chefs and consumers, if you will—need to vote with both their forks and their wallets in support of more diverse and regionally self-sufficient food systems, reducing their carbon foodprints by whatever means they have available to them. But they also need to vote at the ballot box for more climate-friendly food policies.

There has been tremendous momentum in the local food movement over the last two decades, which demonstrates that chefs and consumers *can* generate positive change by selecting foods that are grown with fewer on-farm ecological impacts and fewer transportation miles. And yet our buying power can take us only so far if government policies do not also support climate-friendly alternatives to industrial agriculture. One ugly fact remains: The agricultural commodity groups that remain in denial about climate change have many more lobbyists defending the status quo in food and farm bills than there are lobbyists fostering innovation and diversification of our food system. The farming and food communities need to get smart about encouraging political changes that recruit, retain, and reward more farmers who are willing and able to experiment with new adaptations to change, and to communicate their on-farm experiments to their neighbors. We must vote at the table *and* at the ballot box if we don't want to be caught doing too little too late.

**Principle 4: Climate change is best dealt with as one of many compounding factors disrupting agricultural, ecological, and human health, and not as an environmental impact apart from all others.**

Along the Gulf Coast of Louisiana, we learned that most of the current loss of farmlands was caused not by floods and hurricanes or ocean level rising, but by land subsidence and saltwater intrusion facilitated by pipelines, levees, and road rights-of-way. As we put this book to bed, the *Deepwater Horizon* oil spill, a tragic side effect of our thirst for carbon-based fuel, threatened to kill much of the remaining coastal wetlands vegetation that buffers New Orleans and the rest of the Gulf Coast from storm surges and floods. We can't afford to deal with these problems in piecemeal fashion, with separate task forces on ocean level rising, land subsidence, and pipeline relocation; we need task forces of non-governmental and governmental players charged with protecting and restoring the Gulf Coast through integrated strategies. There will be no farmers—let alone tabasco and cayenne chile farmers—left on the Gulf Coast unless we take a holistic approach to recovering the natural and cultural communities of this vulnerable region.

In addition, there are strong lobbies fighting against any more funding for climate change research, mitigation, and adaptation, but few would dare to oppose a comprehensive plan for restoring the Gulf Coast's open waters, wetlands, and farmlands.

Principle 5: We need to empower local food communities—ones that link farmers, foragers, fishers, and ranchers with chefs, consumers, and educators—to be "co-designers" of  local solutions to global change, and then to creatively transmit their solutions to other communities for adoption, refinement, rejection, or adaptation.

One inherent problem with trying to address global climate change is that the immensity and complexity of the issue tends to disempower some citizens and disable certain kinds of plans for community action. The less confident among us feel like our personal efforts are mere drops in the bucket, and the bucket is not only large but leaking badly. That's why we need to encourage every farmer and consumer to use their creativity to help redesign our food systems. Many of the communities we visited have already begun to overcome this temporary sense of powerlessness and have initiated projects that can indeed make a change in our food system, which, after all, has been a major contributor to carbon emissions and ultimately to global warming. There is not a top-down or one-size-fits-all solution to this issue. No silver bullets, please! And climate change is too important to our lives and those of our descendants to leave it up to the government or the scientific priesthood. Instead, we need a billion on-the-ground innovators, and a million street preachers encouraging participation, not despondency. In particular, we need to empower networks of youth to design do-it-yourself solutions that reduce greenhouse emissions and carbon food-prints. Get your creative juices flowing!

• • •

We will leave you with just these few principles as "for instance" examples, but we encourage you to add your own. Three gastronauts don't have all the answers. All we can possibly offer you are some stories that indicate that climate change is something that farmers, gardeners, chefs, and eaters have the capacity to deal with—with creativity, wit, and wisdom—and that the solutions lie within *you*.

# LITERATURE CITED

## Introduction and General References

Andrews, J. 1995. *Peppers: The Domesticated Capsicums.* University of Texas Press, Austin.

————. 1999. *The Pepper Trail: History and Recipes from Around the World.* University of Texas Press, Austin.

Anonymous. 2009. Agriculture and food supply. www.epa.gov/climatechange/effects/agriculture.html.

Bosland, P. W. 1994. Chiles: history, cultivation and uses. In *Spices, Herbs and Edible Fungi,* edited by George Charalambous. Elsevier Publications, New York.

————. 1996. Capsicums: innovative uses of an ancient crop. In *Progress in New Crops,* edited by J. Janick. ASHS Press, Arlington, VA.

————. 1999. Chiles: a gift from a fiery god. *Hort Sci* 34:809–811.

Cichewicz, R. H., and P. A. Thorpe. 1996. The antimicrobial properties of chile peppers (*Capsicum* species) and their uses in Mayan medicine. *J Ethnopharma* 52:61–70.

Collier, M., and R. H. Webb. 2002. *Floods, Drought and Climate Change.* University of Arizona Press, Tucson.

DeWitt, D. 2010. The soul of Mexicans, part 2. http://blog.mexgrocer.com/the-soul-of-the-mexicans-part-2.

DeWitt, D., and N. Gerlach. 1990. *The Whole Chile Pepper Book.* Little, Brown, New York.

Eshbaugh, W. H. 1963. Role of cultivation in the evolution of *Capsicum. Am J Bot* 50:633–635.

————. 1993. Peppers: history and exploitation of a serendipitous new crop. Pages 132–139 in *New Crops,* edited by J. Janick and J. E. Simon. Wiley, New York.

Faris, S. 2009. *Forecast: The Consequences of Climate Change.* Henry Holt, New York.

Gore, Albert. 2007. *An Inconvenient Truth.* Rodale Press, New York.

Grondine, Tracy Taylor, and Mace Thornton. 2010. Stallman to ag critics: circumstances have changed. Farm Bureau Voice of Agriculture. www.fb.org/index.php?file=nr0110.html.

Harlan, J. 1992. *Crops & Man.* Crop Sciences Society of America, Madison, WI.

Hass, M. 1994. The ethnobotany of *Capsicum* in some New World societies. Master's thesis, University of Montana.

Heiser, C. B. 1976. Peppers—*Capsicum* (Solanaceae). Pages 265–268 in *Evolution of Crop Plants,* edited by N. W. Simmonds. Longman, London, England.

Kolbert, E. 2006. *Field Notes from a Catastrophe: Man, Nature and Climate Change.* Bloomsbury Books, London, England.

Kraft, K. H. 2009. The domestication of the chile pepper, *Capsicum annuum*: genetic, ecological and anthropogenic patters of genetic diversity. PhD thesis, University of California–Davis.

Lappé, Anna. 2010. *Diet for a Hot Planet: The Climate Crisis at the End of Your Fork and What You Can Do About It.* Bloomsbury USA, New York.

McKibben, B. 2006. *The End of Nature,* 2nd ed. Random House Trade Paperbacks, New York.

Perry, L., R. Dickau, S. Zarrillo, I. Holst, D. M. Pearsall, D. R. Piperno, M. J. Berman, R. G. Cooke, K. Rademaker, A. J. Ranere, J. S. Raymond, D. H. Sandweiss, F. Scaramelli, K. Tarble, and J. A. Zeidler. 2007. Starch fossils and the domestication and dispersal of chili peppers (*Capsicum* spp. L.) in the Americas. *Sci* 315:986–988.

Perry, L., and K. V. Flannery. 2007. Precolumbian use of chili peppers in the valley of Oaxaca, Mexico. *Proc Nat Acad Sci USA* 104:11905–11909.

Pickersgill, B. 1977. Taxonomy, origin and evolution of cultivated plants in the New World. *Nature* 268:591–595.

Smith, B. D. 1997. Reconsidering the Ocampo caves and the era of incipient cultivation in Mesoamerica. *Lat Am Antiq* 8:342–383.

———. 2005. Reassessing Coxcatlan Cave and the early history of domesticated plants in Mesoamerica. *Proc Nat Acad Sci USA* 102:9438–9445.

Strom, R. G. 2007. *Hot House: Global Climate Change and the Human Condition.* Springer Publishing, New York.

Truena, Kerry 2010. Snow doubt: what's behind climate change denials? www .huffingtonpost.com/kerry-trueman/snow-doubt-whats-behind-c_b_469359.html.

## Chapter 1. Finding the Wildness of Chiles in Sonora

Hernandez-Verdugo, S., R. G. Guevara-Gonzalez, R. F. Rivera-Bustamante, and K. Oyama. 2001. Screening wild plants of *Capsicum annuum* for resistance to pepper huasteco virus (PHV): presence of viral DNA and differentiation among populations. *Euphytica* 122:31–36.

Hernandez-Verdugo, S., R. Luna-Reyes, and K. Oyama. 2001. Genetic structure and differentiation of wild and domesticated populations of *Capsicum annuum* (Solanaceae) from Mexico. *Plant Syst Evol* 226:129–142.

Hernandez-Verdugo, S., K. Oyama, and C. Vazquez-Yanes. 2001. Differentiation in seed germination among populations of *Capsicum annuum* along a latitudinal gradient in Mexico. *Plant Ecol* 155:245–257.

Holden, W., J. H. Kelley, and R. Moisés. 1969. *A Yaqui Life: The Personal Chronicle of a Yaqui Indian.* University of Nebraska Press, Lincoln.

Nabhan, G. P. 1978. Chiltepines! *El Palacio* 84(2):30–34.

Nabhan, G. P., and P. Mirocha. 1985. *Gathering the Desert.* University of Arizona Press, Tucson.

Nabhan, G. P., M. Slater, and L. Yarger. 1989. New crops for small farmers in marginal lands? wild chiles as a case study. Pages 19–26 in *Agroecology and Small Farm Development,* edited by M. A. Altieri and S. B. Hecht. CRC Press, Boca Raton, FL.

Olivares Duarte, E. 2009. *El Sabor de Sonora.* Editorial Imágenes de Sonora. Hermosillo, SON.

Oyama, K., S. Hernandez-Verdugo, C. Sanchez, A. Gonzalez-Rodriguez, P. Sanchez-Pena, J. A. Garzon-Tiznado, and A. Casas. 2006. Genetic structure of wild and domesticated populations of *Capsicum annuum* (Solanaceae) from northwestern Mexico analyzed by RAPDs. *Genet Resourc Crop Ev* 53:553–562.

Perramond, E. 2005. The politics of ecology: local knowledge and wild chili collection in Sonora, Mexico. *J Lat Am Geog* 4.1:59–75.

Tewksbury, J. J., G. P. Nabhan, D. Norman, H. Suzan, J. Tuxill, and J. Donovan. 1999. In situ conservation of wild chiles and their biotic associates. *Cons Biol* 13:98–107.

Votava, E. J., G. P. Nabhan, and P. W. Bosland. 2002. Genetic diversity and similarity revealed via molecular analysis among and within an in situ population and ex situ accessions of chiltepin (*Capsicum annuum* var. *glabriusculum*). *Cons Gen* 3:123–129.

White, Brian. 2009. Sonoran communities struggle with Hurricane Jimena. KOLD News 13. www.kold.com/Global/story.asp?S=11102305.

## Chapter 2. The Datil Pepper: First Chile of the First Coast

Andrews, J. 1995. A botanical mystery: the elusive trail of the datil pepper to St. Augustine. *Fl Hist Q,* Fall:132–147.

———. 1999. *The Pepper Trail: History and Recipes from Around the World.* University of North Texas Press, Denton.

Carlson, S. 2009. Sustainability can be delicious. *C Higher Edu,* November 22. http://chronicle.com/article/Sorry-Tom-We-Have-to-Eat-You/49231.

Doggett, C. 1919. *Andrew Turnbull and the New Smyrna Colony of Florida.* Drew Press, Jacksonville, FL.

Lawson, E. W. 1937. Interesting information on the arrival of datil pepper in St. Augustine, its growth and uses, is given. *St. Augustine Record,* June 13:4.

Nabhan, G. P., editor. 2008. *Renewing America's Food Traditions.* Chelsea Green Publishing, White River Junction, VT.

Nolan, D. 2009. Letter to Gary Nabhan and Native Seeds/SEARCH from 30 Park Terrace Drive, St. Augustine, FL, August 6.

Rawlings, M. K. 1942. *Cross Creek Cookery*. Charles Scribner's Sons, New York. Reprinted in 1970 as a Fireside Book by Simon & Schuster, New York.

Villadoniga, R. 2010. Datil peppers: heat with a history. Fiery-Foods.com, Embudo, NM. www.fiery-foods.com/article-archives/85-chile-history/2872-datil-peppers -heat-with-a-history?showall=1.

Zanger, M. H. 2003. *The American History Cookbook*. An Oryx Book/Greenwood Press, Westport, CT.

## Chapter 3. Hard Times and Habaneros in the Yucatán

Anderson, E. N. 2006. *Mayaland Cuisine: The Food of Maya, Mexico*. Privately published by the author, Seattle.

Gerlach, N., and J. Gerlach 2002. *Foods of the Maya: A Taste of the Yucatán*. University of New Mexico Press, Albuquerque.

Gerlach, N., and D. DeWitt. 1995. *A Habanero Cookbook*. Little, Brown, New York.

Miller, L. 2003. *A Mayan Kitchen: Regional Recipes from Mexico's Mundo Maya*. Pelican Press, Gretna, LA.

Nabhan, G. P. 2008. *Arab/American: Landscape, Culture and Cuisine in Two Great Deserts*. University of Arizona Press, Tucson.

Neri, N. 1998. *Cocina Yucateca*. Selector Actualidades Editorial, Mexico, DF.

## Chapter 4. Tabascos: A Cure for That Sinking Feeling in Cajun Country

Anonymous. 1901. *The Picayune's Creole Cook Book*. *New Orleans Picayune*. Reprinted in 2002 by Dover Publications, Mineola, NY.

Bernard, S. 2007. *Tabasco: An Illustrated History*. McIlhenny Company, Avery Island, LA.

Burke, J. L. 2007. *The Tin Roof Blowdown*. Simon & Schuster Pocket Books, New York.

Doré, E. M., and M. R. Bienvenu. 2002. *Eula Mae's Cajun Kitchen*. Harvard Commons Press, Boston.

Holland, G.J., and P. J. Webster. 2007. Heightened tropical cyclone activity in the North Atlantic: natural variability or climate trend? *Philosophical Transactions of Royal Society A*. 365(1860): 2695-2716.

Keim, B. D., and R. A. Muller. 2009. *Hurricanes of the Gulf of Mexico*. Louisiana State University Press, Baton Rouge.

Schweid, R. 1999. *Hot Peppers: The Story of Cajuns and Capsicum,* rev. ed. University of North Carolina Press, Chapel Hill.

Shevory, K. 2007. This family's hot stuff. *New York Times,* March 30. www.nytimes .com/2007/03/30/business/31tabasco.web.html.

Tidwell, M. 2003. *Bayou Farewell: The Rich Life and Tragic Death of Louisiana's Cajun Coast*. Vintage Departures, New York.

Webster, P. J., G. J. Holland, J. A. Curry, and H.-R. Chang. 2005. Changes in tropical cyclone number, duration, and intensity in a warming environment. *Science,* 16 September 2005: 1844–46.

## Chapter 5. Strings of Chiles Like Rosary Beads Along the Rio Grande

Alvino, A., M. Centrizzi, and F. DeLorenzi. 1995. Photosynthetic response of sun-lit and shade pepper (*Capsicum annuum*) leaves at different positions in the canopy under two water regimes. *Austr J Plant Physiol* 21(3):377–391.

Anonymous. 2007. *Climate Change and Water: Is New Mexico Vulnerable? A Final Report for Public Forums on Water Policy.* National Commission on Energy Policy and the New Mexico Office of the State Engineer, Santa Fe.

Cuvelier, M. I. n.d. *Saving the Native New Mexican Chiles.* Fiery-Foods.com, Embudo, NM. www.fiery-foods.com/chiles-around-the-world/83-usa/1970-embudo-nm -saving-the-native-new-mexican-chiles.

DeWitt, D. n.d. *The New Mexico Landrace Question.* Fiery-Foods.com, Embudo, NM. www.fiery-foods.com/chiles-around-the-world/83-usa/1970-embudo-nm-saving -the-native-new-mexican-chiles.

Gutzler, D. S. 2007. Climate change and water resources in New Mexico. *New Mexico Earth Matters* 7(Summer).

Hall, T. Y., and R. T. Skaggs. 2002. *New Mexico's Chile Pepper Industry: Chile Types and Product Sourcing.* New Mexico Chile Task Force. Report 8.

Minnis, Paul E., and Michael E. Whalen. The first prehispanic chile (*Capsicum*) from the US Southwest/northwest Mexico and its changing use. *Am Antiq* 75(2):245–262.

State of New Mexico Agency Technical Work Group. 2005. *Potential Effects of Climate Change in New Mexico.* www.nmenv.state.nm.us/aqb/cc/Potential_Effects_Climate_ Change_NM.pdf.

Traverso, A. 2007. Chile season: visit northern New Mexico in September and you'll find a region steeped in tradition, local pride, and the smell of freshly roasted chiles. *Sunset,* September.

Votava, E. J., J. B. Baral, and P. W. Bosland. 2005. Genetic diversity of chile (*Capsicum annuum* var. *annuum* L.) landraces from northern New Mexico, Colorado, and Mexico. *Econ Bot* 59:8–17.

## Chapter 6. A Peek at Our Pick of Imperiled Peppers

Bradshaw, G. I. 2007. Historian traces slave foods to Frederick. *Frederick (MD) News-Post,* March 28. www.fredericknewspost.com/sections/archives/display_detail .htm?StoryID=66654.

Carlson, S. 2010. On the trail of the fish pepper, Baltimore's historic hot stuff. Eat the Prodigal Pepper. *Urbanite Magazine* 71(May 10).

Chloupek, O., P. Hrstkova, and P. Sweigert. 2004. Yield and its stability, crop diversity and adaptability and response to climate change . . . *Field Crops Res* 85:167–190.

Hall, H. F. 1901. *300 Ways to Cook and Serve Shell Fish, Terrapin and Green Turtle.* Christian Banner Print, Philadelphia.

Hatch, P. J. 1998. *The Gardens of Thomas Jefferson's Monticello.* Thomas Jefferson Memorial Foundation, Charlottesville, VA.

Howard, B. C. 1881. *Fifty Years in a Maryland Kitchen: 403 Authentic Regional Recipes.* J. P. Lippincott, Philadelphia.

Nabhan, G. P., editor. 2008. *Renewing America's Food Traditions.* Chelsea Green Publishing, White River Junction, VT.

National Conference of State Legislatures, Center for Integrated Environmental Research, and the University of Maryland. 2008. Illinois: Assessing the costs of climate change. *Climate Change and the Economy.* National Conference of State Legislatures, Washington D.C.

Organic Seed Alliance. 2010. Agriculture and abrupt climate change. Literature review on crop diversity and climate change. http://sites.google.com/site/ents288food/the-organic-seed-alliance/assesing-crop-diversity.

Staub, J. E. 2005. *Seventy-five Exciting Vegetables for Your Garden.* Peregrine Smith Books/Gibbs Smith Publishing, Layton, UT.

Wander, M., and S. Clemmer. 2005. *Impacts on Agriculture: Our Region's Vital Economic Sector.* Union of Concerned Scientists, Washington, DC.

Weaver, W. W. 2009. Fish peppers: spice up your garden with these unique, popular peppers. *Mother Earth News,* April–May.

Whealy, K., and J. Thuente. 1999. *Garden Seed Inventory,* 5th ed. Seed Savers Exchange, Decorah, IA.

# INDEX

*Note: Bold page numbers indicate recipes; page numbers followed with c indicate the Color Insert*

# ABOUT THE AUTHORS

**From left to right: Nabhan, Kraft, Friese**  (Photo credit: Kim McWane Friese)

**CHEF KURT MICHAEL FRIESE** is author of *A Cook's Journey: Slow Food in the Heartland* (Ice Cube, 2008) and owner and founding chef of Devotay, a restaurant in Iowa City that is a community leader in local and sustainable cuisine. He is owner and publisher of *Edible Iowa River Valley Magazine*, a board member of Slow Food USA and the Iowa Food Systems Council, and a graduate and former chef-instructor at the New England Culinary Institute. **KRAIG KRAFT** is an agroecologist and writer based in Managua, Nicaragua. He completed his PhD on the origins and diversity of wild and domesticated chile peppers at the University of California, Davis. Kraft is the author of a popular blog titled *Chasing Chiles* and has written for several regional magazines, including *Edible Sacramento*, as well as technical journals, and is currently working on a coffee sustainability project in Central America. **GARY PAUL NABHAN** is an award-winning natural-history writer and ethnobotanist, recognized by *Mother Earth News* and *Time* as a pioneer in the local foods movement. His collaborative conservation work as been honored with lifetime achievement awards from the Quivira Coalition and the Society for Conservation Biology, and with the Vavilov Medal. A pioneer in heirloom seed saving, he raises rare chile peppers and Mission-era orchard crops in Patagonia, Arizona.

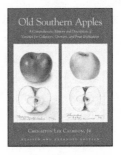

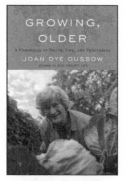
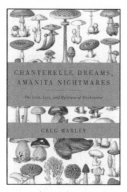